GREAT FOOTBALL HEROES

A HISTORY OF SOCCER LEGENDS OF YESTERYEAR

GREAT FOOTBALL HEROES

A HISTORY OF SOCCER LEGENDS
OF YESTERYEAR

Geoff Tibballs

MICHAEL O'MARA BOOKS

First published in Great Britain in 2003 by
Michael O'Mara Books Limited
9 Lion Yard, Tremadoc Road
London SW4 7NQ

A CIP catalogue record for this book is available from the British Library

ISBN 1-84317-045-0

1 3 5 7 9 10 8 6 4 2

Designed and typeset by Design 23

www.mombooks.com

Printed and bound in Singapore by Tien Wah Press

CONTENTS

Roberto Baggio	10	Diego Maradona	62
Gordon Banks	12	Lothar Matthäus	64
Franz Beckenbauer	14	Stanley Matthews	66
George Best	16	Guiseppe Meazza	68
Danny Blanchflower	18	Roger Milla	70
John Charles	20	Bobby Moore	72
Bobby Charlton	22	Gerd Müller	74
Johan Cruyff	24	Daniel Passarella	76
Kenny Dalglish	26	Pele	78
William 'Dixie' Dean	28	Michel Platini	80
Alfredo Di Stefano	30	Ferenc Puskas	82
Duncan Edwards	32	Roberto Rivelino	84
Eusebio	34	Gianni Rivera	86
Tom Finney	36	Paolo Rossi	88
Garrincha	38	Ian Rush	90
Jimmy Greaves	40	Juan Schiaffino	92
Ruud Gullit	42	Uwe Seeler	94
Jairzinho	44	Peter Shilton	96
Alex James	46	Frank Swift	98
Pat Jennings	48	Marco Van Basten	100
Kevin Keegan	50	Billy Wright	102
Denis Law	52	Lev Yashin	104
Tommy Lawton	54	Zico	106
Gary Lineker	56	Dino Zoff	108
Dave Mackay	58	Brazil	110
Paolo Maldini	60	Acknowledgements	112

INTRODUCTION

There are few quicker ways of starting an argument than asking someone to name their top fifty footballers of all time. Ask a thousand people and you will get a thousand different lists. Some names – Pele, Eusebio, Best, Charlton, Maradona, Beckenbauer, Cruyff – select themselves automatically but what of the rest? Who is to say that Marco Van Basten was a more dangerous striker than Just Fontaine, France's record-breaking goalscorer from the 1958 World Cup?

West German forward Karl-Heinz Rummenigge powers a header towards the Chilean goal during the 1982 World Cup. West Germany beat Chile 4-1.

Or that Gary Lineker was a more accomplished forward than Italy's Luigi Riva? Or that 'Dixie' Dean was better than West Germany's Karl-Heinz Rummenigge? Different styles and eras make it so difficult to compare individual talents. Rather like being an international team manager, it is an almost impossible job.

But I've given it a shot and what I can promise is that within these pages you will find mini biographies of fifty of the greatest footballers of all time – men who were not only superb sportsmen but were also true heroes in the eyes of fans. From Aberdeen to Buenos Aires, every club has its heroes. They may not necessarily be the best players, but often people whose commitment to the cause has endeared them to

Italy's Luigi Riva (right) is challenged by West Germany's Karl-Heinz Schnellinger (on ground) and Berti Vogts during the 1970 World Cup. Italy won 4-3 after extra time.

supporters. Consequently, I have included the likes of Alex James, Frank Swift, Tommy Lawton and Dave Mackay. Each possessed immense talent even though, in terms of international caps, their records were not exceptional. Above all, they were revered wherever they played, their exploits lovingly recounted to subsequent generations. A near miss in this area was Bert Trautmann, Manchester City's legendary goalkeeper of the 1950s, the man who famously broke his neck during the 1956 FA Cup Final but carried on playing to help City defeat Birmingham 3-1. A former German prisoner of war, Trautmann had not exactly been welcomed at Maine Road in 1949 at a time when his fellow countrymen were still viewed with considerable suspicion in Britain. Fans even threatened to boycott games in protest at the club signing a German. Yet by his sheer courage he won over those same fans to become an unlikely hero.

Inevitably, the restriction of numbers creates unwanted omissions. As a boy of nine I well remember watching the 1960 European Cup Final between Real Madrid and Eintracht Frankfurt on black and white

TV. The outstanding team in Europe, Real won 7-3 that night in a match that was the finest advert for football imaginable. Yet it was not Puskas or Di Stefano, Real's star marksmen, who caught my imagination but their left-winger Francisco Paco Gento who created many of the goals with his astonishing bursts of speed down the flank. No one else on the pitch during that match could keep up with Gento, who went on to make nearly 800 appearances for Real and win 43 caps for Spain. But I had to leave him out of the final line-up in favour of even more deserving causes. Many others met a similar fate – the aforementioned Riva and Rummenigge; Brazil's star of the 1938 World Cup, Léonidas; Republic of Ireland and Arsenal playmaker Liam Brady; Sandor Kocsis who averaged over a goal a game alongside Puskas for the great Hungarian national team of the 1950s; England's Nat Lofthouse and Bryan Robson. The list goes on.

I have deliberately refrained from including footballers who are still in their prime, the only current players to feature being Roberto Baggio and Paolo Maldini, both of whom are nearing the ends of long and illustrious careers. Beckham, Ronaldo and Zidane can wait for a future edition.

Instead, relive the silky skills of Platini, Garrincha and Schiaffino; the old-fashioned wing trickery of Matthews and Finney; the defensive solidity of Moore, Wright and Passarella; the safe hands of Banks, Yashin and Zoff; and the striking instincts of Müller, Gullit and Dalglish. Every one a great football hero.

GEOFF TIBBALLS

Opposite: *Manchester United and Real Madrid captains Denis Law and Francisco Gento lead their teams out onto the pitch.*
Above: *Bolton Wanderers and England centre-forward Nat Lofthouse.*

ROBERTO BAGGIO

ROBERTO BAGGIO

There are nicknames and there are nicknames. 'The Black Panther' (Eusebio), 'Der Kaiser' (Franz Beckenbauer) and 'The Vulture' (former Spanish international striker Emilio Butragueno) conjure up images of power and composure. But 'The Divine Ponytail'? All that can be said about a footballer who revels in such an absurd moniker is that, to do so, he must be a very talented player indeed.

That is certainly the case with Roberto Baggio, a slim forward with pace and finesse who, at his peak, was as accomplished as any player in the world – good enough in the eyes of Italian fans to warrant the adjective 'divine'.

Baggio was born in Caldogno and started his career with local club Vicenza in 1982 at the age of fifteen. After thirteen goals in 36 games, he was transferred to Fiorentina in 1985 for his first taste of Serie A football. It was in Florence that he started to demonstrate his true potential and in season 1988-89 he won his first international cap, scoring 24 goals in 40 Italian League and Cup games. He followed up with another seventeen League goals in 1989-90, putting Fiorentina under pressure to sell their hottest property to one of the big clubs in the north. The inevitable move came in the summer of 1990 shortly before the World Cup on home soil when Juventus paid a world record fee of £7.7 million for Baggio. His departure sparked off three days of rioting in the streets by angry Fiorentina fans.

People outside Italy could see what all the fuss was about when the World Cup got underway. Against Czechoslovakia Baggio ran half the length of the pitch and turned several players inside out before shooting past the keeper. Italy were eventually knocked out in the semi-finals by Argentina but Baggio had arrived on the world stage.

He spent five successful seasons with Juventus, scoring 79 League goals in 141 games and helping the club to win the UEFA Cup in 1993 and the Serie A title two years later. He was also voted both European Footballer of the Year and World Footballer of the Year in 1993. The only low point came when he was substituted against Fiorentina in 1991 after refusing to take a penalty against his old club.

The Italians started the 1994 World Cup with their customary sloth but it was Baggio who woke the team from its slumbers by scoring two crucial goals against Nigeria to keep his country in the competition. Another against Spain in the quarter-final and then two in the semis against Bulgaria meant that he had dragged Italy virtually single-

Roberto Baggio

Born: Caldogno, Italy, 1967

Country: Italy

International Caps: 55

International Goals: 27

Position: Striker/Midfield

Clubs: Vicenza, Fiorentina, Juventus, AC Milan, Bologna, Inter Milan, Brescia

handed to the final. Alas, that was where it all went wrong. When a dour goalless encounter with Brazil went to a penalty shoot-out, Baggio blazed his kick high over the bar and sank to his knees in despair. Brazil were world champions for the fourth time.

Somewhat unfairly, national coach Arrigo Sacchi made Baggio the scapegoat for Italy's defeat and omitted him from future squads despite overwhelming public and media campaigns for his inclusion. After failing to agree a new contract with Juventus in 1995, he moved to AC Milan for £10 million and, although he spent much of his time on the bench, played his part in Milan's League title success, making him only the third player in Italian history to win a championship medal with different clubs in successive seasons. In 1997 he joined relegation strugglers Bologna and scored 22 goals to push them to a UEFA Cup place but he then endured a miserable two years with Inter Milan before joining his current club, Brescia, in 2000. By the end of January 2003 his career total stood at 189 goals in 302 games. Even at 36 there is still plenty of life and bounce in 'The Divine Ponytail'.

Roberto Baggio on the ball for Brescia against Bologna in 2002.

GORDON BANKS

GORDON BANKS

Pele called it 'the greatest save I had ever seen.' And he had a closer view than most. For it was his superbly directed downward header from Jairzinho's cross, looking a goal from the second it left his head, that sent England goalkeeper Gordon Banks plunging to his right to scoop the ball to safety at the foot of the post. The incident has since been replayed countless times on television and has rightly been hailed as the Save of the Century. Brazil went on to win that World Cup group match 1-0 but the reputation of the man they called Banks of England was well and truly cemented.

Yet what would turn out to be such a glittering career had started inauspiciously. Despite playing for Sheffield Boys, Banks had no intention of making a living from the game and instead became a coalman's mate and then an apprentice bricklayer. And when he did play for a local amateur side – Romarsh Welfare of the Yorkshire League – he was axed after only two games during which he had conceded no fewer than fifteen goals. This was the man who would go on to keep 35

clean sheets in 73 internationals and was on the losing side for England just nine times.

Fortunately salvation was at hand in the form of Chesterfield who signed the 22-year-old as a part-time professional on £2 a match in 1955. Following two years of National Service, he resumed his career with the Spireites, playing 23 League games as a full-time professional before joining Leicester City for £7,000 in 1959. The pain of two FA Cup Final defeats for his new club was eased by success in the Football League Cup in 1964 and his international call-up. He made his debut against Scotland at Wembley in April 1963, replacing Ron Springett in what was Alf Ramsey's second game in charge. It was a baptism of fire, England going down 2-1 to the Auld Enemy – Scotland's first win in London for 12 years.

With Banks between the posts, England had a firm base on which to build their 1966 World Cup campaign. He didn't concede a goal until the semi-final (against Portugal) but then it looked as if West Germany's last-minute equaliser in the final might cruelly snatch glory from him. Banks later recalled: 'It was like being pushed off Mount Everest with just a stride to go to the top.' But as history records, he and his team-mates made it to the summit in extra-time.

Although England's undisputed number one, his club position was about to come under threat from a 17-year-old by the name of Peter Shilton and, barely ten months after the World Cup triumph, Banks was allowed to move to Stoke City for £52,500. He remained Ramsey's first choice but the 1970 World Cup in Mexico was to end in recriminations and no little intrigue when Banks mysteriously went down with a stomach bug on the eve of the quarter-final with West Germany. His deputy, Peter 'The Cat' Bonetti, kept goal more like a dopey kitten and England bowed out.

Awarded the OBE in 1970, Banks was named Footballer of the Year two years later – the first goalkeeper to win the honour since his schoolboy hero Bert Trautmann picked up the award in 1956. Also in 1972 he helped Stoke win their first major trophy (the Football League Cup) but the year was to end in disaster when he lost the sight in his right eye following a horrific car crash. In that instant his career was all but finished.

He did a spot of coaching and then signed for Fort Lauderdale Strikers in the North American Soccer League where, despite his handicap, he was voted most valuable goalkeeper in his first season. But he hated the razzmatazz. 'I felt like a circus act,' he said. 'Roll up, roll up, to see the greatest one-eyed goalkeeper in the world.'

Pele would have sympathised.

Opposite: *Gordon Banks saves England from Scotland's Denis Law at Wembley in 1965.*
Above: *The first ever official World Cup mascot, Willie the lion, appeared in 1966.*

Gordon Banks

Born: Sheffield, England, 1937

Country: England

International Caps: 73

International Goals: 0

Position: Goalkeeper

Clubs: Chesterfield, Leicester City, Stoke City, Fort Lauderdale Strikers

FRANZ
BECKENBAUER

FRANZ BECKENBAUER

Franz Beckenbauer stands alone in the annals of football – the one man to win the World Cup both as a captain and a manager. As a player, he led West Germany (as they were then known) to victory on home soil in 1974 and sixteen years later completed a unique double by managing the team that defeated Argentina 1-0 in Rome.

Yet there was much more to Beckenbauer than mere statistics. Even those who considered the German game to be robotic and physical, paling in comparison alongside the flamboyant Brazilians, were forced to admit that Beckenbauer had style. Upright, elegant and unruffled, he strode across the turf in a manner that suggested he owned every blade of grass. He exemplified German superiority – some would say arrogance – as he pioneered the role of the attacking sweeper. Before Beckenbauer, defenders only ventured forward for set pieces but he had the confidence, the audacity, to carry the ball from the back on long powerful runs with an authority that almost dared the opposition to tackle him. No wonder they called him 'Der Kaiser'. England came to regret Beckenbauer's development more than any other nation as it was his surge forward, culminating in a speculative shot, that brought the Germans back into the 1970 World Cup quarter-final. From a seemingly impregnable 2-0 advantage, England crumbled to bow out of the tournament 3-2 – a result that raised the first question marks against the tactical expertise of Sir Alf Ramsey.

Beckenbauer was born amid the ruins of post-war Germany on 11 September 1945. At the age of fourteen he joined the youth team at his local club, Bayern Munich, and three years later relinquished his job as a trainee insurance salesman to become a professional footballer. He made his first-team debut in 1964 as an outside-left but was soon switched into midfield and within a year had won his first international cap in a vital World Cup qualifying win in Sweden. Arguably, the 1966 finals came too soon for him. Although he scored four times *en route* to the final, he was unable to contain Bobby Charlton in the match that mattered. Beckenbauer himself later reflected: 'England beat us in 1966 because Bobby Charlton was just a bit better than me.'

His revenge came four years later by which time he had also guided Bayern to domestic and European honours, including a 1967 European Cup Winners' Cup final success against Glasgow Rangers. In 1971 he was made captain of his country, a role that enabled him to perfect the sweeper role. At the following year's European Championships

Franz Beckenbauer

Born: Munich, Germany, 1945

Country: Germany

International Caps: 103

International Goals: 14

Position: Midfield

Clubs: Bayern Munich, New York Cosmos

Beckenbauer, revelling in the freedom of being unmarked, became the focal point for every German move and steered his nation to a crushing victory over the Soviet Union in the final. His reward was to be named European Footballer of the Year – a title he also won in 1976. This was truly Beckenbauer's golden age. In addition to the 1974 World Cup triumph, he captained Bayern to three successive European Cups between 1974 and 1976. Under Beckenbauer's influence, Bayern were probably the finest club side in the world.

In 1977 he joined the exodus to the fledgling North American Soccer League, helping New York Cosmos win the Soccer Bowl three times in four years. Despite possessing no coaching experience, he was appointed manager of West Germany in 1984 and proceeded to take an indifferent German team to the World Cup final in 1986 where they lost 3-2 to Argentina. Four years later Beckenbauer's team made amends. His place in history was assured.

Moving into club management, he had a brief and uncharacteristically barren spell with Olympique Marseille before returning to his beloved Bayern in 1994 and leading them to the Bundesliga title. He duly became club president – a role he would occupy with the same grace and polish that he did as a player.

Holland's Johan Cruyff (left) and West Germany's Franz Beckenbauer in action during the 1974 World Cup Final. West Germany won 2-1.

GEORGE BEST

GEORGE BEST

One of George Best's favourite stories against himself was of the time when the man from room service delivered vintage champagne to the fading football genius in his suite at a plush hotel. There was £20,000 in cash scattered on the bed while beneath the sheets was the current Miss Universe. The waiter shook his head sombrely. 'Tell me, Mr Best,' he sighed, 'where did it all go wrong?'

Best would subsequently argue that nothing did go wrong – that he simply got bored with football and fame. But to have seen him at his peak, when his balance, pace and footwork allowed him to do things with a football that even the world's greatest players could only dream of, and then to watch his sad decline into alcoholism, bankruptcy, jail and ill-health . . . sorry, George, but it did go wrong. George Best's story is that of a wasted talent, of a shy Belfast boy who was seduced by the bright lights of London in the Swinging Sixties. He was without doubt the most talented footballer that Britain has ever produced yet he squandered those precious gifts on a steady diet of booze and birds with the result that he spent only six years at the top. It was nothing short of criminal.

Yet it had all started so promisingly. Despite fleeing back to Ulster within 24 hours of his arrival at Old Trafford in 1961, the homesick 15-year-old was persuaded to return to Manchester where his dazzling skills and dribbling ability soon set the grapevine buzzing. He turned professional in 1963, making his debut on the left wing against West Bromwich Albion whose full-back that day was the experienced Welsh international Graham Williams. After being 'nutmegged' early on, Williams was generally given the runaround by the precocious youngster who inspired United to a 1-0 victory. When the two men met some years later, Williams asked Best to stand still for a moment so that he could look at his face. 'Why?' asked a puzzled Best. 'Because all I've ever seen of you,' explained Williams, 'is your arse disappearing down the touchline.'

Williams was in good company. Best went on to score over a century of goals for United, including

George Best

Born: Belfast, Northern Ireland, 1946

Country: Northern Ireland

International Caps: 37

International Goals: 9

Position: Left Wing

Clubs: Manchester United, Stockport County, Fort Lauderdale Strikers, Fulham, Dunstable Town

six in a Cup tie against Northampton Town in 1970. Best said afterwards: 'I was so embarrassed I played the last 20 minutes at left-back.' He helped the club to League titles in 1965 and 1967 and to European Cup glory in 1968, the year in which he was also named European Footballer of the Year. With his dark good looks and Beatle haircut, Best became the first celebrity footballer, receiving 1,000 fan letters a week. Boys may have had posters of Bobby Charlton or Denis Law on their wall; girls had George Best. Perhaps his finest game for the club was a 1965 European Cup tie in Lisbon against the mighty Benfica. Best inspired United to a resounding 5-1 win and was promptly christened 'El Beatle' by the Portuguese press.

But by the early seventies the high life was taking its toll. He regularly skipped training and went missing but if the United backroom team needed to know where he was, they rarely had to look further than the front pages of the tabloid newspapers, for Best's decline was played out in the full public gaze. Effectively washed up at 25, he hung around at United until 1974 before plying his trade at such outposts as Stockport County, Fort Lauderdale Strikers, Dunstable Town and Ford Open Prison, the last courtesy of a drink-driving conviction and an assault on a policeman.

A frail figure following his recent liver transplant, Best has left us with a brief but golden legacy and the inescapable feeling that it could have been so much better had he been able to pass a nightclub the way he passed a ball.

George Best aged 25. His skill as a footballer was ultimately overshadowed by his exploits off the pitch.

DANNY BLANCHFLOWER

When Danny Blanchflower was approached by Eamonn Andrews with his big red book to be told he was about to be the subject of television's *This Is Your Life*, he turned on his heels and ran. Andrews gulped in disbelief; the nation was stunned. The incident became the topic of conversation in pubs and sitting-rooms the length and breadth of the land. After all, nobody had ever snubbed *This Is Your Life*. But that was Danny Blanchflower – single-minded and determined, qualities that made him the inspirational right-half and captain of one of the greatest ever English club sides, the 'Glory Glory' Tottenham Hotspur team of the early sixties.

Robert Dennis Blanchflower was born in Belfast, the eldest of five children. As a football-mad youngster, he would often play three times a day for local teams and even formed his own club, Bloomfield United. In 1943, eager to do his bit for the war effort, he lied about his age and joined the RAF. When the war finished, he was persuaded to leave the RAF and sign professional forms for

Glentoran but on discovering that some of his team-mates were being paid more than the legal maximum, he demanded a transfer and joined Barnsley for £6,000 in 1949. In the same year he made his international debut for Northern Ireland against Scotland at Windsor Park, Belfast. It was not the most promising of starts. The Irish crashed 8-2.

Two years on and Blanchflower was snapped up by Aston Villa for £15,000. He made 148 appearances at Villa Park, scoring 10 goals, but became disenchanted with the club's tedious training routines, which consisted more of lapping the pitch than honing ball skills, and their failure to embrace new continental tactics. When Villa announced in 1954 that he was available for transfer, Arsenal and Spurs became involved in a bidding war. Arsenal, however, refused to go above £28,500 and Spurs got their man for £30,000 – a huge fee in those days for someone of 28. Ever outspoken, Tottenham's new captain frequently fell out with manager Jimmy Anderson and his successor, Bill Nicholson, over tactics. Having been named Footballer of the Year in 1958, he was horrified when Nicholson dropped him. Saying he had no intention of languishing in the reserves, he asked for a transfer but Nicholson soon reinstated him to his rightful position.

With Blanchflower pulling the strings in midfield with his economical but probing passing, Spurs went on to scale unforeseen heights. Winning their first eleven games of the season, in 1961 they became the first team to complete the League and Cup double in the twentieth century. They took the title by eight points and defeated Leicester City at Wembley. They nearly repeated the achievement the following year, but had to settle for third place in the League and another FA Cup success, this time against Burnley. Then in 1963 Blanchflower became the first captain of a British side to lift a major European trophy when Spurs hammered Atletico Madrid 5-1 in the European Cup Winners' Cup Final. Advancing years and a persistent knee injury forced him to retire from the game in 1964. He had made 337 League appearances for Spurs, scoring fifteen goals.

At international level, he led Northern Ireland to their first-ever victory at Wembley in 1957 and then captained the side that reached the quarter-finals of the 1958 World Cup in Sweden. They might have progressed further but for the absence of Blanchflower's brother Jackie who had been seriously injured in the Munich air crash.

On retirement, the erudite Blanchflower became a respected journalist but could not resist putting his ideas into practice. He managed both Northern Ireland and Chelsea in the 1970s but neither post was a success and he returned to his newspaper column. Beset by Alzheimer's Disease, he died in 1993. It was a cruel end for a man of such intelligence and vision.

GREAT FOOTBALL HEROES

DANNY BLANCHFLOWER

Opposite: Spurs Captain Danny Blanchflower holds the FA Cup as he is carried by his team-mates after a 2-0 victory over Leicester City in the 1961 FA Cup Final at Wembley.

Danny Blanchflower

Born: Belfast, Northern Ireland, 1926 (d. 1993)

Country: Northern Ireland

International Caps: 56

International Goals: 2

Position: Right half

Clubs: Glentoran, Barnsley, Aston Villa, Tottenham Hotspur

John Charles

Born: Swansea, Wales, 1931

Country: Wales

International Caps: 38

International Goals: 15

Position: Centre forward/Centre half

Clubs: Swansea, Leeds United, Juventus, Roma, Cardiff City

JOHN CHARLES

Nicknamed 'The Gentle Giant', John Charles was truly a colossus of the game, equally adept at playing centre forward or centre half. Indeed, the 42 League goals that he scored for Leeds United in 1953-54 (still a club record) came at a time when he was playing in defence for Wales. Yet his lasting fame is as British football's first major export to Italy where his achievements surpassed those of the illustrious names that followed him in the early sixties, including proven goalscorers such as Denis Law and Jimmy Greaves. Charles outshone them all, helping Juventus to three Italian Championships and two Italian Cups. He became a hero in a foreign land.

Born in Swansea, he joined the ground staff at his hometown club before moving to Leeds where he made his first-team debut in 1949. The following year he became the youngest player to appear for Wales when, at eighteen years and 71 days, he strode out against Northern Ireland. His record stood until Ryan Giggs stepped on to the

international scene 42 years later. Charles was then a centre half but his powerful physique (he was 6ft 2in tall and weighed nearly fourteen stone) encouraged Leeds to try him out in attack as one of the big, bustling centre forwards that were in vogue at the time. His tremendous heading ability made him an instant success in his new role and by the time he signed for Juventus for a British record fee of £65,000 in 1957, he had scored 150 goals in just 297 appearances for Leeds.

Like George Best, the fact that he represented one of the lesser football nations denied Charles a prominent place on the world stage. Yet there was no denying Charles's pride in playing for Wales, whom he first captained in 1957. And the following year he helped his country reach the World Cup finals for the only time in their history. Exceeding all expectations, Wales drew their three group matches and beat Hungary in a play-off to reach the quarter-finals. There they met the eventual champions Brazil but, despite a gallant effort, Wales went down to a solitary goal from Pele. Significantly, Charles missed that match through injury.

Meanwhile, he was quickly becoming a huge favourite in Turin. The Italian game, built on the principles of a miserly defence, traditionally meant lean pickings for strikers yet Charles managed to score a remarkable 93 goals in 155 games for Juventus. The world's toughest defenders simply could not contain him.

By 1962 Charles and his family were missing home and he returned to Leeds for £53,000. However, he stayed just three months (scoring three times in 11 games) before surprisingly heading off back to Italy to join Roma for £70,000. Sadly, he was a shadow of his former self. That subtle first touch, unusual for such a big man, had deserted him and he had lost some of his pace and power. Sensing that Italian defences had finally got the measure of him, he once again answered the call of home and the following year he joined Cardiff City where he played alongside his younger brother Mel. John Charles retired from League football in 1966 at the end of an illustrious career during which he had averaged a goal every other game.

He briefly tried his hand at management with Hereford United but then drifted out of football altogether, as a publican and shopkeeper. If ever a man lived up to his nickname, it was Charles. For despite the intimidation to which he was subjected by defenders, he was never once sent off or even booked. And to this day he remains a hero, not just in his native Wales (for whom he was arguably their finest ever player), but also in a corner of Italy where he will forever be remembered as 'Il Buon Gigante' – the Gentle Giant.

GREAT FOOTBALL HEROES

JOHN CHARLES

Opposite: *John Charles, playing centre forward for Juventus, battles with Arsenal centre half Bill Dodgin at Highbury.*

BOBBY CHARLTON

BOBBY CHARLTON

Someone wrote that England's exit from the 2002 World Cup was the saddest parting since Bobby Charlton's. And although the sight of those long wisps of hair flowing at right angles from his head as he built up a head of steam was vaguely comical, such considerations were overridden by the undeniable fact that his boots possessed awesome power. In the 1960s there was never a goal quite like a Bobby Charlton goal — sweetly struck, rising, bulging the back of the net from upwards of twenty yards, often before the hapless goalkeeper could move. Furthermore, these spectacular goals were struck with either foot. Bobby Charlton wasn't blighted with the modern curse of having a 'weaker foot'.

But as with most of the true sporting greats, there was so much more to Charlton than simply being a footballer. He was an ambassador for the game, a true gentleman, a firm believer in fair play who never argued with referees and never got into trouble on or off the pitch. In short, he was every youngster's ideal role model.

He was born into a football family in the Northumberland mining village of Ashington. His grandfather and four of his uncles were professional footballers, one of those uncles being the legendary Newcastle and England centre forward 'Wor' Jackie Milburn. Encouraged by his football-mad mother Cissie, Charlton became a frequent visitor to St. James' Park where he studied visiting players such as Stanley Matthews. Charlton later admitted: 'It was from Stan that I learned how to find space, how to beat an opponent, how to put defenders off balance and how to time my runs.'

He signed as a professional with Manchester United in 1954 (scoring twice on his debut against Charlton Athletic) and became one of the famous 'Busby Babes', an outstanding group of young players moulded by manager Matt Busby. However, Busby's dream of creating the greatest club side in Europe was cruelly wrecked in the Munich air crash of 6 February 1958 when seven of the Babes died. Thrown clear of the wreckage, Charlton survived with a cut head and went on to be the key figure as Busby painstakingly rebuilt the United team.

After making his international debut in 1958, his finest moments in an England shirt came in the 1966 World Cup finals where he played alongside elder brother Jack. Three goals in the tournament (including two in the semi-final against Portugal) helped Charlton and England become world beaters. That year he was voted both English and European Footballer of the Year.

Bobby Charlton

Born: Ashington, England, 1937

Country: England

International Caps: 106

International Goals: 49

Position: Midfield

Clubs: Manchester United, Preston North End

At club level he had won his first FA Cup winners' medal in 1963 but eclipsed this in 1968 by scoring two goals (one a rare header) as United finally fulfilled Busby's dream by lifting the European Cup at the expense of Benfica on an unforgettable Wembley night.

Sadly, his England career finished on a low note when England lost 3-2 to West Germany in the 1970 World Cup quarter-finals. Charlton was sitting on the bench at the time, having been controversially substituted by Sir Alf Ramsey with England leading 2-0 and the match seemingly won. Ramsey explained that he had wanted to save Charlton for the semi-final.

Bobby Charlton left Manchester United in 1973, having scored a club record 247 goals in 754 appearances, and joined Preston North End as player/manager but, as others have found out before and since, great players don't automatically make great managers. He duly returned to his spiritual home of Old Trafford as a director and in 1994 received a knighthood for his services to the game.

It was richly earned. As Busby once said: 'There has never been a more popular footballer. He was as near perfection as man and player as it is possible to be.'

Below: *The Charlton brothers Bobby (left) and Jack go head-to-head in a match between Manchester United and Leeds United. Jack's team won 2-1.*
Below left: *A magazine souvenir special for the 1966 World Cup during which Bobby and Jack played alongside each other.*

JOHAN CRUYFF

JOHAN CRUYFF

Among the most enduring footballing images of the 1970s was that of the Dutch master Johan Cruyff standing out on the left wing, the ball at his feet, confronted by a defender, but apparently unsure of his next move. In an instant he suddenly dragged the ball behind him with his right foot, spun through 180 degrees and sprinted away from his bewildered opponent. It was an outrageous trick, the like of which had never been seen before on the international stage. Only the most gifted – and most confident – of players would attempt such a feat. Cruyff was not lacking in either commodity.

He was born in Amsterdam where his mother worked as the original Ajax cleaner and it was she who persuaded the club's coaches to admit her son into their youth development scheme. On the recommendation of the English coach Vic Buckingham, Ajax offered Cruyff professional terms in 1963. Not only did he score on his club debut but he repeated the achievement in his first international in 1966, snatching a last-minute equaliser against Hungary. Under the influence of new coach Rinus Michels, Ajax developed into one of the most feared sides in Europe with Cruyff, by now a supreme athlete, as the lynchpin of their attacking play. The

Johan Cruyff scores the first goal for Holland against Argentina in the 1974 World Cup in Germany.

Johan Cruyff

complete opposite of the traditional English battering ram centre forward, he had vision, pace, exceptional ball control and a licence to roam. He helped Ajax to a hat-trick of European Cup triumphs between 1971 and 1973 and was voted European Footballer of the Year on an unprecedented three occasions (1971, 1973 and 1974). In 1973 he moved to Barcelona for a world record fee of £922,000 and inspired his new team to the Spanish League title in his first season, highlighted by a 5-0 win away to arch rivals Real Madrid.

At international level the Dutch were on the verge of greatness. Equally at home in midfield, attack or on the wing, Cruyff embodied their philosophy of Total Football, which allowed players to switch roles as circumstances dictated. He was not one to hide his light under a bushel and, as captain, was the loudest voice in an outspoken Dutch side. He had actually been banned from the national team for a year after being sent off in only his second game for Holland but at the 1974 World Cup he was determined to channel his energies in the right direction. No defender in the tournament could get to grips with him. The Dutch would have been popular winners of the World Cup but lost out in the final to host nation West Germany. Cruyff was bitterly disappointed and retired from international football before the next World Cup.

After a spell in the North American Soccer League and then in Spain, he rejoined Ajax and led them to two more League titles before making a shock move to their fierce rivals Feyenoord whom he led to the League and Cup double in 1984.

With 215 Dutch League goals to his name, he took up coaching back at Ajax, and guided the club to European Cup Winners' Cup success in 1987. Having walked out on Ajax in a fit of pique, he replaced Terry Venables at Barcelona and captured a remarkable eleven trophies in his eight years in charge, the highlight being the club's eagerly-awaited first European Cup triumph. However, his dictatorial style of management won him as many enemies as trophies and in 1996 he was unceremoniously sacked. Cruyff was that rarity – a great player who became an inspirational, innovative coach. In short, he was a total footballer.

Cruyff lining up Holland's second goal against Brazil as the Dutch side headed for the World Cup final which they lost to host nation West Germany.

Johan Cruyff

Born: Amsterdam, Netherlands, 1947

Country: Holland

International Caps: 48

International Goals: 33

Position: Striker

Clubs: Ajax, Barcelona, Washington Diplomats, Feyenoord

Kenny Dalglish

Born: Glasgow, Scotland, 1951

Country: Scotland

International Caps: 102

International Goals: 30

Position: Centre forward

Clubs: Celtic, Liverpool

Opposite: In his old Liverpool colours, although he was then manager of Newcastle, Kenny treads the turf at Anfield to play in 1998 in a special charity match in aid of the Roy Castle Lung Cancer Foundation.

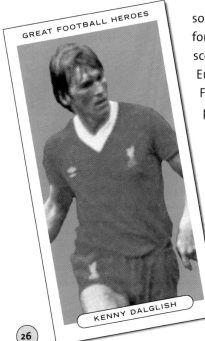

GREAT FOOTBALL HEROES

KENNY DALGLISH

KENNY DALGLISH

When an inquisitive journalist asked Celtic manager Jock Stein whether Kenny Dalglish's best position was in attack or midfield, Stein replied: 'Och, just let him on the park.' That was the thing about Dalglish. He was so comfortable on the ball that he could have played almost anywhere. Nevertheless, he was always at his best with his back to goal on the edge of the box where a sudden swivel of the hips would leave a defender for dead before he curled the ball beyond the despairing keeper into the far corner of the net. He did it so often it virtually became his trademark.

A childhood Glasgow Rangers supporter, he started out playing in goal at primary school but then switched to right-half. He had trials with a number of clubs, including Liverpool, who turned him down after one game for the 'B' team. When Liverpool rectified their mistake eleven years later, it cost them a British record fee of £440,000.

Liverpool's loss was to be Glasgow Celtic's gain. The sixteen-year-old Dalglish signed on at Parkhead in 1967 just as Jock Stein's team were becoming the first British team to lift the European Cup. It took Dalglish three years to establish himself in the first team, by which time Celtic were the undisputed kings of Scottish football. Many a rugged defender tried to kick him off the park, only to learn that he was by no means as fragile as his stature suggested, for Dalglish was not afraid to mix it with the best.

After collecting ten major medals with Celtic and 167 goals, he sought a fresh challenge and moved to Anfield in 1977 as a replacement for the Hamburg-bound Kevin Keegan. Dalglish was an instant success, scoring 30 goals in his first season, among them the winner in the European Cup Final against FC Bruges at Wembley. England's Footballer of the Year in 1979 and 1983, he formed a formidable partnership with Ian Rush who was able to make incisive runs knowing that 'King Kenny', as he became known, would deliver an inch-perfect pass. These were Liverpool's glory years: five League titles, four League Cups and two more European Cups. In 1985 Dalglish became player/manager and in his first season at the helm guided Liverpool to the League and Cup double – a feat that had eluded both Bill Shankly and Bob Paisley. It was no surprise that he was named Manager of the Year.

But with success came sadness – the Heysel tragedy of 1985 and the Hillsborough disaster four years later. The loss of 95 fans in Sheffield left Liverpool a city in mourning, their dignified grief epitomised by Dalglish who described the laying of flowers in the goalmouth at the Kop as 'the saddest and most beautiful sight I have ever seen.' Dalglish hung up his boots that year, having become the first player to score a century of League goals in both England and Scotland. Despite having picked up two more League titles (1988 and 1990) and a hollow FA Cup victory (1989), there were signs that he was beginning to feel the strain. In 1991 he suddenly quit the Anfield hot seat citing the stress of the job, only to return to management eight months later at Blackburn Rovers where in 1995, assisted by owner Jack Walker's millions, he took the Lancashire club to their first League Championship in 81 years. Two years later he had a short, acrimonious stint at Newcastle.

A man of few words (especially to the media), Dalglish is very much his own man. He never showed his true worth at international level (although he is Scotland's joint leading scorer) but his record of thirteen championships as a player and manager in England and Scotland is truly exceptional. Management may be a precarious profession but one certain job for life is to be Kenny Dalglish's trophy polisher.

DIXIE DEAN

WILLIAM 'DIXIE' DEAN

Statistics can be misleading, but not in the case of 'Dixie' Dean. He averaged over a goal a game for England, scored 349 League goals in 399 matches for Everton and in the 1927-28 season amassed a total of 60 First Division goals – a record that still stands and is unlikely ever to be beaten. What's more, he only played in 39 of the 42 League matches that season.

Dean – he apparently hated the nickname 'Dixie' and preferred to be known as William or Bill – started his career across the Mersey with Tranmere Rovers for whom he scored 27 goals in just 29 games. This alerted Everton who signed him in 1925 but his Goodison career was nearly over before it had begun when a motorcycle accident left him unconscious for 36 hours with serious head injuries. Happily he made a complete recovery and in just over a year was embarking on that record-breaking season – a third of his 60 goals coming from headers! Peerless in the air, he could also shoot hard with either foot and was a constant handful for defenders. Going into the final match that season, at home to Arsenal, Dean needed three goals to snatch the scoring record from Middlesbrough's George Camsell who had scored 59 times in Division Two only the season before. To the delight of the Everton crowd, Dean responded with a hat-trick — one of 34 he would score in his career, the most ever by a British player. He also scored 22 goals in other matches that season (three in FA Cup ties, 19 in representative games), bringing his overall total to 82. Not surprisingly Dean's phenomenal goal haul helped Everton lift the First Division Championship.

Background: *Spanish keeper Zamora denies Dixie Dean at Highbury in 1931.*
Inset: *Dean's famous heading ability featured on this stamp.*

FOOTBALL LEGENDS
DIXIE DEAN 1907-1980

William 'Dixie' Dean

Born: Birkenhead, England, 1907 (d.1980)

Country: England

International Caps: 16

International Goals: 18

Position: Centre forward

Clubs: Tranmere Rovers, Everton, Notts County, Sligo Rovers

Even when Everton were relegated two years later, he netted 23 times in 25 games. His 37 goals in 1930-31, including a run of scoring in twelve successive League matches, enabled Everton to bounce back at the first attempt. The following season Dean was again rampant, his 45 goals firing Everton to another League Championship. In 1933 he won a Cup Winners' medal, scoring four times on the way to Wembley and another in the final itself as Manchester City were humbled 3-0. His favourite stage was a Merseyside derby and only Ian Rush has surpassed his total of nineteen goals in matches against Liverpool.

Curiously, he scored his 200th League goal at the age of 23 years and 290 days – exactly the same age as Jimmy Greaves was when he reached that milestone three decades later.

Dean made his international debut in 1927 against Scotland in Glasgow and scored both goals in England's 2-1 victory. He went on to score twelve times in his first five internationals with a sequence of 2, 3, 2, 2 and 3 – not a bad way to begin a career at international level. He played his final game for England against Northern Ireland in 1933, the fact that he won a mere sixteen caps being a tribute to the wealth of talent that was around at the time.

By 1937 Dean's powers appeared to be on the wane and he was allowed to join Notts County but played only nine games before moving to Ireland where he helped Sligo Rovers reach the final of the Irish Cup. He finally retired from playing in 1939, having scored 379 League goals in 437 matches.

A jovial character who enjoyed banter with team-mates and opponents alike, he went on to run a pub for fifteen years. He later worked as a security guard for Littlewoods Pools and then retired to live on the Wirral. He died in 1980, fittingly enough at Goodison Park after collapsing while watching the derby match with Liverpool.

ALFREDO DI STEFANO

ALFREDO DI STEFANO

In the eyes of many judges, Alfredo Di Stefano was the most complete footballer of all time. Physically powerful with unparalleled stamina and supreme skills, he also had an insatiable competitive streak. Francisco Gento, his Real Madrid team-mate in six European Cup finals, said: 'Whenever we practised, even when we played cards or basketball in the gym, he would want to win. When I became a manager I realised how important it was to have a player like that on the field.'

Curiously Di Stefano was capped by three different countries yet never took part in a World Cup. However his other achievements were sufficient to warrant a place among the world's elite.

Born in Buenos Aires of Italian parents, Di Stefano worked on the family farm as a boy and thus acquired the strength that would stand him in good stead on the football pitch and enable him to play at the highest level until he was 40. At the age of twelve, he joined a youth team, Los Cardales, for whom he once scored a hat-trick in just twenty minutes. In 1942 he joined his father's old club River Plate where he went on to lead a legendary forward line known as La Maquina (The Machine), helping his team to two Argentinian Championships. He made his debut for the national side in 1947 but two years later moved to Millonarios of Bogota to play in the outlawed Colombian League, powering the team to four League titles and personally scoring an amazing 267 goals in 294 games. He won two Colombian caps before moving on to Spain in 1953 to join the club with whom he would enjoy his finest years – Real Madrid.

Real had never previously won a major trophy but their ambitious president, Santiago Bernabeu, had built a magnificent stadium and needed a team of superstars in order to fill it with spectators. He wanted to make Real the most powerful club in Europe and, to fulfil his dream, recruited the best player in South America, Di Stefano. He made his debut against none other than Barcelona, scoring four times in a 5-0 drubbing. Bernabeu had reaped an instant reward on his investment.

The balding Argetinian turned Real from Spanish nonentities into the biggest club on the planet. The all whites were unstoppable, due in no small part to Di Stefano's ability to alternate between midfield and attack. One moment he was scoring goals, the next he was creating chances for the likes of Gento and Ferenc Puskas. With Di Stefano scoring in every final (including a hat-trick against Eintracht Frankfurt), Real won a historic five successive European Cups (1956-60). He scored

Alfredo Di Stefano

Born: Buenos Aires, Argentina, 1926

Country: Argentina, Colombia, Spain

International Caps: 40

International Goals: 30

Position: Midfield

Clubs: River Plate, Millonarios of Bogota, Real Madrid, Español

49 goals in his 56 games in the tournament, a record that still stands. As well as helping Real collect eight Spanish League titles, he finished top scorer in the Spanish League on five occasions and was named European Footballer of the Year in 1957 and 1959. He also managed 23 goals in only 31 internationals for his third country, Spain.

Released unharmed after being kidnapped on a 1963 tour of Venezuela, he joined Español in 1964 but ended his playing career two years later. He went on to coach a number of teams (Boca Juniors, Sporting Lisbon, River Plate, Valencia and Real Madrid) with varying success, the highlight being steering Valencia to their first Spanish title in 24 years.

But it is as a player that he will always be remembered. Matt Busby summed up Di Stefano's immense talent. 'He was one of the greatest, if not the greatest footballer I had ever seen. At that time we had forwards and defenders doing separate jobs, but he did everything.'

Di Stefano scores one of his hat-trick of goals for Real Madrid against Eintracht Frankfurt in the European Cup final at Hampden Park in 1960. Real won 7-3.

DUNCAN EDWARDS

The mere mention of the name 'Duncan Edwards' is enough to bring a wistful sigh from even the most hardened soccer fan over the age of 60. For Edwards, who was just 21 when he died, was widely considered to be the outstanding English player of his generation, an immense talent who would surely have gone on to conquer at all levels. Whereas George Best effectively finished his own career, Edwards' was ended for him – by the Munich air crash of 1958.

The problem with assessing the merits of Duncan Edwards is that because of his short career, relatively few people actually saw him play. Furthermore, British television was still fairly primitive at the time with the result that there are few reminders of his special powers available on tape. In such tragic circumstances there is always the risk that a player's worth can be exaggerated out of sentiment – in the same way that Marc Bolan is now regarded as a rock icon – so in Edwards' case it is best to let the facts speak for themselves.

He was born in Dudley on 1 October 1936 and by the age of eleven was the star player in the town's boys' team, despite

A victim of the Munich air crash of 1958, Duncan Edwards' talents were never fully realised.

playing against predominantly fifteen-year-olds. A giant for his age and with the strength to match, his raw talent quickly alerted a posse of Football League clubs desperate to secure his signature. Although he had joined Manchester United as an amateur at the age of fifteen, others were trying to poach him and so United coach Bert Whalley drove through the night to arrive at the Edwards' house at daybreak on the birthday that 'Big Dunc' was eligible to turn professional. Rousing the boy from his bed, Whalley had the ink on the contract dry before breakfast.

GREAT FOOTBALL HEROES

DUNCAN EDWARDS

He made his United debut on Easter Monday 1953 against Cardiff City. At sixteen years and 185 days old, he was then the youngest player ever to turn out for the club. His deft touch, relentless energy, aerial command and thunderous shooting soon established him as a First Division player, principally as a strong left-half although he occasionally led the attack in an emergency. It was only a matter of time before he represented his country, doing so in 1955 in a 7-2 demolition of Scotland. Edwards was just eighteen years and 183 days old – the youngest player ever to play for England until Michael Owen broke on to the scene in 1998.

Mature beyond his years, he was the youngest member of the 'Busby Babes' team that won the League title in 1956 — an achievement United repeated the following year. Edwards' only disappointment was missing out on a deserved League and Cup double in 1957 when United lost in the final to Aston Villa, having been reduced to ten men through an injury to goalkeeper Ray Wood. But the championship success enabled United to make a second foray into Europe. The Football Association frowned on European competition (it had banned the 1955 champions, Chelsea, from taking part) but Busby was not to be dictated to. United had just clinched a semi-final place when their world fell apart on that snowbound afternoon in Munich.

Edwards clung to life for 15 days after the crash. Thousands prayed that he would pull through; surely he was indestructible. But in the end the injuries were too much even for his mighty body to endure. Ironically, had he lived and continued playing at left-half, Bobby Moore may never have got a look in.

Jimmy Murphy, United's assistant manager, described Edwards as 'the Kohinoor diamond amongst our crown jewels,' adding that, 'he remained an unspoiled boy to the end, his head the same size it had been from the start.' Bobby Charlton paid the ultimate tribute: 'If I had to play for my life and could take one player with me it would be Duncan Edwards.' That's how good he really was.

Duncan Edwards

Born: Dudley, England, 1936 (d 1958)

Country: England

International Caps: 18

International Goals: 5

Position: Left half

Clubs: Manchester United

Eusebio outleaps England's Nobby Stiles during the 1966 World Cup semi-final.

EUSEBIO

Eusebio da Silva Ferreira is the most famous footballer that Portugal has ever produced. He has been the subject of a film, *Sua Majestade o Rei* (*His Majesty the King*), is fêted wherever he goes and in 1992 a statue in his honour was unveiled outside Benfica's Stadium of Light. Small wonder when you consider that in 291 League games for the Lisbon club he scored an incredible 317 goals, many of them spectacular.

Eusebio had grace, pace and power, earning him the nickname of 'The Black Panther'. His deadly shooting allied to his strong running and dribbling skills made him one of the most dangerous strikers in the world. At the height of his fame in the sixties he was hailed as Europe's Pele.

As a teenager in the Portuguese colony of Mozambique, Eusebio was a sprint champion and an accomplished basketball player, but football was the game he loved. He made his debut in 1958 with Lourenço Marques, a nursery club for Portuguese giants Sporting Lisbon, but Benfica were also alerted to Eusebio's talents when their coach, Bela Guttmann, happened to be sitting in the hairdresser's next to the coach of Brazilian club Sao Paolo, who were touring Portugal at

the time. The Brazilian told Guttmann about a brilliant footballer he had seen in Portuguese East Africa and within a week Guttmann had flown out to sign Eusebio. Unfortunately Sporting still thought they had a claim on him too and so when Eusebio arrived in Lisbon in 1961 he was 'kidnapped' by Benfica and hidden away in an Algarve fishing village until the two clubs settled their differences!

With the contract wrangle eventually resolved in Benfica's favour, Eusebio made an instant impact, helping the club win the Portuguese title in his first season. The following year he scored twice as Benfica humbled five-times winners Real Madrid 5-3 in the European Cup Final in Amsterdam – the first time Real had tasted defeat in a major European final. In 1963 he again scored in the European Cup Final but this time Benfica slipped up 2-1 to AC Milan at Wembley. He went on to play in two more finals – against Inter Milan in 1965 and Manchester United in 1968 – but finished on the losing side both times.

Voted European Footballer of the Year in 1965, Eusebio was already an established international by the time of the 1966 World Cup. He was without doubt the outstanding player of the tournament, being top scorer with nine goals, including four in that epic encounter with North Korea where he single-handedly dragged the Portuguese back from the very brink of an embarrassing defeat. Despite also scoring in the semi-final defeat against England, he left the pitch in tears. His performances had made such an impression on the British public that his figure was immediately added to Madame Tussaud's waxwork collection. Most defenders must have wished they had been playing against the dummy.

His speciality right-foot thunderbolts made him the leading scorer in Portugal on seven occasions and his total of 46 goals in European competition put him second only to Alfredo Di Stefano. In addition he twice finished top scorer in the whole of Europe with 42 goals in 1968 and 40 in 1973. By the time he left Benfica to move to the newly formed North American Soccer League in 1975 following a bad knee injury, he had picked up no fewer than ten Portuguese League winner's medals. In his fifteen seasons in Lisbon, there were only two in which he failed to win a major honour.

After two years in America he returned to Benfica as coach but, as so often happens, he failed to repeat his success as a player. In his entire career he played 715 games and scored 727 goals. He was truly awesome.

Eusebio

Born: Lourenço Marques (now Maputo), Mozambique, 1942

Country: Portugal

International Caps: 64

International Goals: 41

Position: Striker

Clubs: Benfica, Boston Minutemen, Toronto Metros-Crotia, Las Vegas Quicksilver

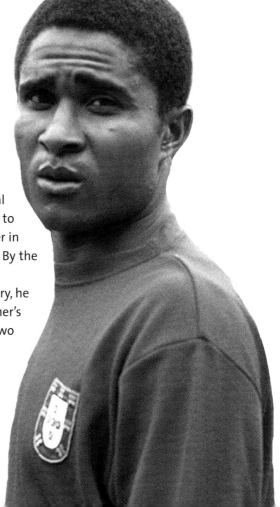

Tom Finney

Born: Preston, England, 1922

Country: England

International Caps: 76

International Goals: 30

Position: Winger/Centre forward

Clubs: Preston North End

TOM FINNEY

In the 1950s you were either a Finney man or a Matthews man. There wasn't room for both, at least not in the eyes of the FA selection committee who met to pick the England teams. Both were players of outstanding ability but unfortunately they were often vying for the same wing position. The debate as to who was the better player divided the nation. However, on caps alone, Finney emerged the winner, not least because he was more adaptable and able to play not only on either wing but just about anywhere along the forward line.

Tom Finney was a throwback to the days when players turned out for a pittance and remained loyal to one club throughout their career. In Finney's case, the lucky beneficiaries were Preston North End. Raised a stone's throw from their Deepdale ground, he yearned to play for the local team but his father insisted that he learn a trade and so he

became an apprentice plumber – an occupation that he kept even when he was an established international. It earned him his nickname of 'The Preston Plumber'.

He signed for North End in 1938 at the age of sixteen but because of the war did not make his first League appearance for another eight years. In 1947 he made his international debut against Wales but thereafter found himself in almost constant competition with Matthews. The latter was undoubtedly the greater showman, teasing full-backs before jinking to the byline and delivering a telling cross, but the feeling was that Finney was the better team player. As well as being blessed with pace and trickery, he had two good feet and could either go outside his full-back to deliver a cross or cut inside for a shot on goal. Matthews may have been a superb provider but Finney was a far more lethal marksman, averaging thirteen League goals a season at Preston and doubling that tally in 1957-58. Unfortunately, Preston were one of the 'nearly teams' of the fifties, twice finishing runners-up in the League and losing out to West Bromwich Albion in the 1954 Cup Final. As a result, the only domestic honour Finney had to show for such a glorious career was a Second Division Championship medal. Compensation of a sort was the accolade of being the first person to be named Footballer of the Year twice.

He was offered the chance of a move – and untold wealth – at the age of 30 when Italian club Palermo put in a bid for him. They were willing to pay a £10,000 signing on fee, £130 a month wages, bonuses of up to £100 a game, a Mediterranean villa, a luxury car and free travel to and from Italy for his family. They also offered Preston £30,000 by way of a transfer fee. Finney turned it down. It would have meant giving up his plumbing business.

Dogged by injury in his later years, Finney retired in 1960, having scored 187 League goals in 433 appearances for Preston. Without him North End were relegated from the First Division within a year and haven't been back since. The perfect gentleman on and off the pitch and a wonderful ambassador for the game, he received the OBE in 1961 and was later elected president of Preston North End. Then in 1998 he received a long overdue knighthood.

So who was better, Finney or Matthews? That shrewd judge Bill Shankly had no doubt. 'Tommy Finney was grizzly strong. Tommy could run for a week. I'd have played him in his overcoat . . . When I told people in Scotland that England were coming up with a winger who was better than Stanley Matthews, they laughed at me. But they weren't bloody laughing when big Georgie Young was running all over Hampden Park looking for Tommy Finney!'

GREAT FOOTBALL HEROES

TOM FINNEY

Opposite: *Tom Finney (left) outwitting Geoff Thomas in a match between Preston North End and Nottingham Forest.*

GREAT FOOTBALL HEROES

GARRINCHA

GARRINCHA

As a child Garrincha had both legs crippled by polio, the disease leaving him with a left leg that bent inwards and a right one that was two and a half inches shorter and curved outwards. But it didn't stop him from playing football and he went on to be acclaimed the world over for his electric pace and brilliant dribbling. Bizarrely his deformed knee joints were almost designed for curling shots struck with the outside of the foot and it was the swerving banana shot which would become his trademark.

Manuel Francisco dos Santos was born into poverty in Pau Grande, a small city near Rio de Janeiro. He joined his local club in 1947, remaining with them for six years before turning professional with Botafogo. There he was given the nickname 'Garrincha' (meaning 'Little Bird'), songbirds being one of his favourite hobbies . . . along with women and alcohol. On the pitch, the frail winger wasted no time in showing off his dazzling skills. He marked his first appearance by scoring a breathtaking hat-trick in the 6-3 victory over Bonsucesso and went on to score 232 goals in 581 games in his thirteen-year stay with Botafogo. During that period the most eagerly awaited games in Brazilian domestic football were invariably the encounters between Garrincha's Botafogo and Pele's Santos – meetings of two of the world's most exciting talents. In these epic contests the little man in the number seven shirt proved every bit the equal of his more illustrious compatriot.

Garrincha first played for his country in 1955 – against Chile – and was a member of the 1958 World Cup squad that travelled to Sweden. He had to wait until the third group game for his big chance in the tournament, the team doctor having told Vicente Feola, the Brazilian coach, that including Garrincha in the team would be a disaster. However, the players pleaded with Feola to include the 'Little Bird' and Garrincha confounded his critics by hitting the bar in the first minute against the USSR. He and the other newcomer in that game, Pele, made all the difference to Brazil's attack and eventually inspired their country to a 5-2 victory over the host nation in the final.

The next World Cup proved even more successful for Garrincha as it allowed him to emerge from Pele's shadow. With Pele injured in only the second game in Chile, Garrincha was thrust into the limelight. He responded by switching from his usual wing position to centre forward and scoring two brilliant goals in the 3-1 quarter-final victory over England, both the result of outrageous individualism. He then scored

Garrincha

Born: Pau Grande, Brazil, 1933 (d.1983)

Country: Brazil

International Caps: 51

International Goals: 13

Position: Right wing

Clubs: Botafogo, Corinthians, AJ Barranquilla, Flamengo, Red Star Paris

two more in the semi-final with Chile, only to blot his copybook by getting sent off for retaliation in the 84th minute. As he left the pitch he was hit by a bottle thrown from the crowd. Following a personal plea to FIFA from the Brazilian President, Garrincha was given clearance to play in the final where he picked up a second World Cup winners' medal as Czechoslovakia were beaten 3-1.

At the 1966 World Cup in England, Garrincha made an early impact by scoring with a curling free-kick in the 2-0 win against Bulgaria. But with Pele rested for the second game against Hungary, Brazil crashed 3-1, Garrincha limping off after being the victim of a hard tackle. It would be his last international and was the only time he played on the losing side for Brazil.

He played for a handful of Brazilian clubs over the next few years but, besieged by marital and financial problems, slipped into a rapid decline and died in 1983 of alcohol poisoning at the age of 49.

There is a saying in Brazil – 'Pele was the best, but Garrincha was better.' And even Pele acknowledged: 'Without Garrincha, I would never have been a three times world champion.'

The Brazilian team, led by Garrincha (second from right), parade their flag in the very first of such celebrations after beating Sweden 5-2 in the 1958 World Cup final.

JIMMY GREAVES

Jimmy Greaves was the most accomplished goalscorer of his generation. An Artful Dodger of a player, he picked defenders' pockets before homing in on goal and was always at his best when he could see the whites of the keeper's eyes. He never went for power but preferred to use his pace, dribbling skills and coolness under pressure to take the ball around the goalkeeper before calmly stroking the ball into the net to inflict maximum humiliation. Outside the penalty area his work was negligible; inside he was lethal.

Greaves began his career with Chelsea on 23 August 1957, scoring on his debut against Tottenham. The next month he went one better, netting twice in his first game for England Under-23s against Bulgaria. His speed of thought and lightning reactions kept the goals flowing for Chelsea at an unbelievable rate. He scored five times in a game on three occasions and reached 100 League goals for the club in just 133 appearances – the first man to pass the century mark in League football before the age of 21. His total of 41 League goals in the 1960-61 season set a Chelsea record that stands to this day. His prowess had been recognised by the England hierarchy and in 1959 he made his international debut versus Peru, again scoring in a 4-1 victory. His popularity at Stamford Bridge meant that there was outrage when the lure of the lira took him to AC Milan for £80,000 in the summer of 1961.

Naturally, he scored on his Italian debut but, despite bagging nine goals in fourteen games, he failed to settle and jumped at the chance to return to England four months later. Spurs manager Bill Nicholson paid £99,999 for his services because he didn't want to burden his star with being Britain's first £100,000 footballer. Continuing his tradition of scoring on debuts, he snatched a hat-trick against Blackpool and went on to help Spurs to FA Cup success at the expense of Burnley. Then, in 1963, he scored twice in Spurs' 5-1 victory over Atletico Madrid in the European Cup Winners' Cup Final – the first European trophy to be won by an English club. His 37 League goals for Tottenham that season meant that he held the scoring record for two London clubs at the same time.

Jimmy Greaves

Born: London, England, 1940

Country: England

International Caps: 57

International Goals: 44

Position: Striker

Clubs: Chelsea, AC Milan, Tottenham Hotspur, West Ham, Barnet

He was equally prolific at international level, scoring eleven goals in five internationals in 1961, including a hat-trick in England's 9-3 annihilation of Scotland. He played in the 1962 World Cup and was expected to make a big impact in the 1966 tournament. However, his form seemed to desert him and after two lacklustre performances he was injured against France. Although his replacement, Geoff Hurst, excelled, the fit-again Greaves was confident of being recalled for the final. Alf Ramsey had other ideas. Hurst kept his place and achieved immortality with the hat-trick that crowned England as world champions. Unpopular though his decision may have been with the public, Ramsey had been thoroughly vindicated. A depressed Greaves boycotted the victory party. It was not his finest hour.

GREAT FOOTBALL HEROES

JIMMY GREAVES

He made his final England appearance in 1967 against Austria and three years later was transferred to West Ham as part of the deal that took Martin Peters to White Hart Lane. Inevitably he scored on his debut, poaching two goals against Manchester City to maintain a remarkable sequence. His Upton Park days were not his happiest and in 1971 he made the shock decision to retire from the game at just 31 years of age with 357 Football League goals to his name.

Opposite and left: Jimmy Greaves pictured in training with Spurs in 1967 and '69. Below: Greaves' image was used on this 1966 World Cup commemorative stamp, although he never played in the final.

But he was rarely out of the headlines, teaming up with Ian St John to front the soccer magazine programme *Saint and Greavsie* and enduring a well-chronicled battle against alcoholism. He also tried his hand at being a chat show host . . . the result being enough to drive anyone to drink.

4d ENGLAND WINNERS

World Cup 1966

HARRISON AND SONS LTD

RUUD GULLIT

RUUD GULLIT

The dreadlocked Ruud Gullit was one of those wonderfully versatile Dutch players who appeared comfortable in just about any position on the pitch. He could play sweeper, in midfield or centre forward. He would probably have even done a decent job in goal.

Gullit's secret was his athleticism. He was able to cover ground without ever appearing to hurry and, like all great players, always seemed to have more time than those lesser mortals around him. Gullit oozed class, and class players don't need to rush. And for a tall man, he also possessed a surprisingly delicate touch, which enabled him to bring team-mates into the game with subtle flicks and lay-offs.

Born in Amsterdam, he played for Meerboys as a junior before being spotted by former West Bromwich Albion player Barry Hughes, then the coach of Haarlem. Gullit signed for Haarlem in 1978 and went on to play 91 League games for the club, scoring 32 goals. He made his international debut on his nineteenth birthday but ended up on the losing side as Holland went down 2-1 to Switzerland. In 1982 he moved to Feyenoord where, despite often playing as a sweeper, he still managed to register 30 goals in 85 League appearances. It was on moving to PSV Eindhoven for £400,000 in 1985 that he was pushed into the forward line, and revelling in his new role, scored 46 goals in 68 League games to help his team to two successive League titles and attract the attention of the leading European clubs.

Another move was inevitable and in 1987 he signed for AC Milan for a world record fee of £6.5 million. That year he was voted both the European and the World Footballer of the Year, only the third player – after Paolo Rossi and Michel Platini – to achieve the double. Gullit dedicated the awards to the imprisoned Nelson Mandela.

In 1988 he became the first captain to lead Holland to international success when they beat the Soviet Union 2-0 in the final of the European Championships. Gullit got the all-important first goal with a powerful header. In the same year he steered Milan to their Italian League title in nine years. The following year he scored twice as Milan beat Steaua Bucharest 4-0 in the European Cup final and was duly voted World Footballer of the Year for a second time.

He recovered from a serious knee injury to help Milan retain the European Cup in 1990 and picked up two more League titles with Milan before joining Sampdoria in 1993. In total he had played 117 League games for Milan, scoring 35 goals. Repeated disagreements with

Ruud Gullit

Born: Amsterdam, Netherlands, 1962

Country: Holland

International Caps: 65

International Goals: 16

Position: Striker/Midfield

Clubs: Haarlem, Feyenoord, PSV Eindhoven, AC Milan, Sampdoria, Chelsea, Newcastle United

national coach Dick Advocaat saw Gullit walk out of the team's training camp three weeks before the 1994 World Cup, bringing a premature end to his international career. Further brief spells with Milan (three goals in eight games) and Sampdoria (nine in 22) prefaced a move to England when he joined Chelsea in 1995, progressing to player/coach upon Glenn Hoddle's appointment as England manager. Although he missed much of the 1996-97 season with an ankle injury, he still helped Chelsea win the FA Cup, in the process becoming not only the youngest manager to lift the Cup but also the first non-British manager to win a major trophy in England. However, he was sensationally sacked by the Stamford Bridge club in 1998 after contract talks broke down amidst allegations that he was behaving like a playboy. Much in demand, he soon took over at Newcastle, promising to bring 'sexy football' back to St. James' Park. The honeymoon didn't last.

A cool, laid-back character with a flair for reggae, he has in his time shared a stage with both Paul Simon and Frank Sinatra. Certainly when Ruud Gullit the footballer was on song there were few better sights to behold.

Ruud Gullit in 1995, playing against Everton in his first Premiership game for Chelsea following his arrival from Italy.

JAIRZINHO

JAIRZINHO

At the start of the 1970 World Cup, all eyes were on Brazil's star player, Pele. By the end the talk was of another Brazilian maestro, the explosive Jairzinho, who created history by becoming the only man to score in every round of a World Cup finals tournament.

A tall, fast, direct right-winger, Jairzinho was seen as the natural successor to Garrincha. He may have lacked the dribbling skills of the 'Little Bird' but his expert control, shrewd runs and powerful shooting still made him one of the most feared strikers in the world.

Jair Ventura Filho was born in Rio de Janeiro on Christmas Day 1944. As a thirteen-year-old he joined Botafogo where Garrincha reigned supreme. Consequently Jairzinho started out on the left wing for the club and occasionally played at centre forward until an injury to Garrincha allowed him to switch to the right.

He made his debut for the national side in 1964 against Portugal and played in all three games at the 1966 World Cup, which ended with Brazil literally being kicked out of the competition by the tough tackling Hungarians and Portuguese. Although he failed to score in that tournament, his time was only four years away.

At one stage a serious injury had threatened his career but he came to Mexico in prime form. He showed his intentions in Brazil's opening game by conjuring up two marvellous individual goals in the 4-1 thrashing of Czechoslovakia. For his first he flipped the ball over the onrushing Czech keeper and then slammed it into the empty net and for his second he evaded two sliding tackles before firing low into the corner of the goal. Brazil's second match was against England and it was Jairzinho who finally settled the game by racing on to Pele's clever pass and driving past Gordon Banks from a narrow angle. When Jairzinho scored again in the next game – a 3-2 win over Romania – opponents suddenly realised there was more to worry about than Pele in the Brazilian attack. After scoring in the quarter-final with Peru, he produced another individual goal in the 3-1 victory over Uruguay in the semis. Italy were swamped 4-1 in a memorable final, Jairzinho bundling in the third to take his tournament tally to seven and more importantly to seal that place in the record books.

A broken leg in 1971 kept him on the sidelines for several months but when he had fully recovered he decided to try his luck in Europe with Marseille. It was a miserable period in his life and, beset by a loss of form and a spate of disciplinary problems, he returned to Brazil

Jairzinho

Born: Rio de Janeiro, Brazil, 1944

Country: Brazil

International Caps: 82

International Goals: 34

Position: Right wing

Clubs: Botofoga, Marseille, Cruzeiro, Portuguesa

after little more than a year.

By the time the 1974 World Cup came around, Brazil had lost many of their most influential players such as Pele, Tostao and Gerson and proved no match either for the robust Germans or the fluent Dutch. Unrecognisable not only in his new Afro hairstyle but also in a centre forward position, Jairzinho struggled along with his team-mates. Starved of real goalscoring opportunities, he managed to find the target in the unconvincing 3-0 victory over Zaire and also in the 2-1 win against Argentina but defeat to Holland consigned Brazil to the third place play-off, which they lost 1-0 to Poland.

He retired from international football shortly afterwards, his goal total putting him second at the time behind only Pele. On the domestic front he helped Cruzeiro win the South American Club Cup, the Copa Libertadores, in 1976 before ending his career with the Venezuelan club Portuguesa. However, the man who was the star marksman in arguably the finest ever football team – Brazil's 1970 World Cup winners – maintained his links with Cruzeiro and in the early 1990s recommended a talented thirteen-year-old to the club. The boy's name was Ronaldo.

Jairzinho in action against Poland during the 1974 World Cup. Brazil lost 1-0.

ALEX JAMES

Alex James was a legend in baggy shorts. The diminutive Scottish inside-forward was the inspiration behind the all-conquering Arsenal team of the 1930s, helping the Gunners to win four League titles and two FA Cups during his eight years at Highbury. With the possible exception of 'Dixie' Dean, no player of his day attracted more press coverage. If journalists weren't drooling over his sublime ball skills, they were writing about those shorts.

The comical shorts and flapping shirtsleeves made James instantly recognisable. He had adopted the look early in his career after being shown a cartoon of himself drawn by Tom Webster in the *Daily Mail* in which he was depicted with shorts down to his knees. Thereafter James decided to live up to this caricature by always wearing shorts that almost reached the tops of his socks.

James was born in Mossend, Lanarkshire, and raised in the small

Alex James scores for Arsenal against Huddersfield Town at Wembley in the 1930 FA Cup final.

mining village of Beshill. The area was an unemployment blackspot but James was fortunate enough to obtain a job at the local steelworks. After playing for assorted junior clubs, he joined Glasgow team Ashfield at the age of nineteen and while there was spotted by a Raith Rovers director who signed him for the Kirkcaldy club for the start of the 1922-23 season. James soon settled in, playing well enough to earn an invitation to play in a Scottish trial along with his close friend Hughie Gallacher. James scored 27 goals in 100 games for Raith before being transferred to Preston North End in 1925 for a fee of £3,000. His form at Preston – he would eventually score 53 goals in 147 matches for the club – won him his first Scottish international cap against Wales in 1926 but his outstanding performance was as part of the 'Wembley Wizards' who destroyed England 5-1 at Wembley in 1928. James tormented the England defence that day, weighing in with two goals. His reputation was made.

James fell out with Preston when manager Alex Gibson refused to release him for another Scotland game and Arsenal's Herbert Chapman swooped to sign him for £8,750 in June 1929. There had been a queue of clubs for his signature but Chapman won the day by lining James up with a £250-a-year job as a sports demonstrator at Selfridges department store. The financially astute James deemed this a nice little earner on top of his maximum wage of £8 a week.

He made a slow start to his Highbury career but came good in the 1930 FA Cup Final against Huddersfield Town who had been the team of the 1920s. James scored one goal and made the other as Arsenal won 2-0 to claim their first major trophy. The game raised James's profile yet further. A celebrity at Selfridges, he had his own ghosted newspaper columns and lived something of a playboy existence, attending late night clubs and parties and dressing in elegant clothes. He was a far cry from most footballers of his day.

James's importance to Arsenal can be gauged by the fact that of the 200 games he played between August 1930 and May 1937 he only finished on the losing side in 36. His goal tally – 27 in 261 games for Arsenal – was unremarkable but he was the finest schemer of his day and his imaginative passing created countless chances for the likes of David Jack, Jack Lambert, Joe Hulme and Cliff Bastin. In the 1930-31 season alone, Arsenal racked up 127 First Division goals to win the League Championship by seven points. With James as the focal point of the team, the Gunners kept piling up the trophies but all good things come to an end and in 1937 he was forced to retire following a succession of injuries. He was a tough act to follow – that colourful little character in the baggy shorts.

GREAT FOOTBALL HEROES

ALEX JAMES

Alex James

Born: Mossend, Scotland, 1901 (d. 1953)

Country: Scotland

International Caps: 8

International Goals: 3

Position: Inside forward

Clubs: Raith Rovers, Preston North End, Arsenal

PAT JENNINGS

PAT JENNINGS

Opposite: *Pat Jennings kept a clean sheet against England at Wembley to take Northern Ireland to the 1986 World Cup.*

Pat Jennings

Born: Newry, Northern Ireland, 1945

Country: Northern Ireland

International Caps: 119

International Goals: 0

Position: Goalkeeper

Clubs: Newry, Watford, Tottenham Hotspur, Arsenal

Asked whether his veteran goalkeeper Pat Jennings had a weakness, Arsenal coach Don Howe scratched his head for a moment before suggesting: 'He might be a bit vulnerable to a hard low shot from the edge of the six-yard box!'

It was a fair assessment because Jennings had the lot. Big, strong and agile, his expertise at using his frame to advance from his line and narrow the angle must have made the goal seem the size of an ice hockey net to opposing forwards. Then there were those huge hands with which he used to pluck the ball out of thin air, his speciality being the spectacular one-handed catch just as the ball appeared to be drifting beyond him. Yet for all his attributes, he was the most mild-mannered, softly spoken, unassuming man. He was no stereotypical eccentric goalkeeper. He didn't bawl at defenders like Peter Schmeichel or juggle the ball on the halfway line like Peru's Ramon Quiroga, the player they called, with some justification, 'El Loco' ('The Crazy One'). The closest Pat Jennings came to irregular behaviour was when he scored against Manchester United in the 1967 Charity Shield with a colossal kick that travelled the length of the field before bouncing over the head of opposing keeper Alex Stepney and into the net.

Jennings first entered football as a part-timer with Northern Ireland outfit Newry in 1961, sometimes combining playing with a job in a timber yard. Working with hatchets and hacksaws was hardly compatible with being a goalkeeper. As Jennings himself remarked: 'Most of the sawyers I knew had the top of a finger missing.' In 1963 Jennings' promise between the sticks alerted Watford for whom he played 48 games before joining Tottenham the following year for £27,000 as successor to Scottish international Bill Brown. Also in 1964 while still with Watford he made his international debut against Wales.

For someone who appeared unflappable, he was surprisingly tense before and during a match. He once revealed: 'The concentration put into a game is so high at this level. Often, after a game, I suffer headaches. The pressure is more intense for a goalkeeper. One mistake can cost you the game. Outfield players can make as many mistakes as they like, but keepers cannot, they dare not.'

Jennings conquered his nerves to help Spurs collect four trophies during his thirteen-year stay at White Hart Lane – the FA Cup (2-1 against Chelsea in 1967), the League Cup twice (2-0 against Aston Villa in 1971 and 1-0 against Norwich City in 1973) and the UEFA Cup, 3-2 on aggregate in the all-English affair with Wolves in 1972. He also picked up the Footballer of the Year award in 1973. After 472 League games for Tottenham, he was surprisingly allowed to join North London rivals Arsenal for a bargain £45,000. As Sol Campbell can testify, it is not always an easy move to make.

With Arsenal he appeared in three successive FA Cup Finals although he was on the winning side only once, against Manchester United in 1979. The big Irishman became as popular at Highbury as he had been at White Hart Lane, illustrated by the fact that his testimonial between the two clubs raised £100,000. In 1985 he eventually made way for John Lukic.

Having played in the 1982 World Cup finals, he had a chance to repeat the experience in Mexico — even though he had not played senior club football for over a year — and on his 41st birthday he appeared in his 119th and last game for Northern Ireland against Brazil. That remained a world record for international caps until Peter Shilton passed the total in 1990.

Pat Jennings had one more claim to fame. At the 1980 FA Cup Final he became one of the few goalkeepers in history to let in a header from West Ham's Trevor Brooking.

Kevin Keegan

Born: Armthorpe, England, 1951

Country: England

International Caps: 63

International Goals: 21

Position: Striker

Clubs: Scunthorpe United, Liverpool, SV Hamburg, Southampton, Newcastle United

KEVIN KEEGAN

It was once written of Kevin Keegan that he wasn't fit to lace George Best's drinks. Whilst he lacked the natural skills and trickery of the Irishman, Keegan compensated for these by sheer application and determination, which ultimately gave him a more fulfilling playing career than that of the wayward Best.

Short, sharp and a cool finisher, he created and scored numerous goals for club and country over a sixteen-year period. He was England's superstar of the seventies and early eighties although in all honesty the competition for that title was not fierce.

Born in Armthorpe, Yorkshire, his first job on leaving school was as a clerk with Peglers Brass Works in Doncaster. Ironically he couldn't get into the works first team, being kept out by an assortment of fitters and welders. Further rejection followed before the seventeen-year-old was taken on by Scunthorpe United, for whom he scored a modest seventeen goals in 120 games. Nevertheless, his promise had caught the eye of a number of clubs but while others hesitated, Bill Shankly took the plunge and signed Keegan for Liverpool for £35,000 in 1971. It was to prove one of his most astute captures.

Shankly had signed Keegan principally as a midfielder or an outside-right, but the new boy's form when thrown up front in a pre-season friendly persuaded Shankly to partner him in attack with the lanky John Toshack for the start of the 1971-72 season. Keegan marked his debut by scoring after just twelve minutes against Nottingham Forest and the 'little and large' duo went on to terrorise defences throughout England and Europe, laying on goals for each other almost at will with Keegan using his darting pace to get on the end of Toshack's clever headed flicks. And for a little fella, Keegan himself was no slouch in the air.

He helped Liverpool win the League title and the UEFA Cup in 1973, the year in which he also made his international debut, scoring twice against Wales. He picked up an FA Cup winners' medal in 1974, followed by further League Championships in 1976 and 1977, a second UEFA Cup in 1976 and the biggest prize of all, the European Cup, in 1977. No wonder Liverpool fans saw him as a lucky talisman.

So it came as a nasty shock when, after 68 goals in 230 League games, the club agreed to sell him to SV Hamburg for £440,000 immediately after that European Cup Final in Rome. His goals enabled Hamburg to win the Bundesliga in 1979 and reach the European Cup Final in 1980 where they lost to Nottingham Forest. To add to his

GREAT FOOTBALL HEROES

KEVIN KEEGAN

Footballer of the Year award from 1976, he was twice named European Footballer of the Year (in 1978 and 1979) – the first English player to win it twice.

Keegan returned to England in 1980 to join Southampton (37 goals in 68 League games) and then Newcastle United in 1982 (48 goals in 78 League games). He was so popular on Tyneside that after his last game for the club he was whisked away by helicopter, still in his kit, amid police fears of crowd congestion.

He captained England 31 times, bowing out of international football when he was dropped after the 1982 World Cup finals.

A mercurial character, he bounced back in 1990 as manager of Newcastle where his brand of exciting attacking football sealed his place as a local hero. The city was in mourning when he suddenly resigned in 1997. After a successful spell in charge at Fulham, he took on the England job but his tactical naivety cost him dear and he quit in 2000 following a World Cup qualifying defeat to Germany. He returned to the game the following season as manager of Manchester City and immediately took them back into the Premiership with that familiar cavalier style. It really has been an eventful career – and that's even without the pop single and the perm.

Kevin Keegan, seen here in 1980, captained England 31 times.

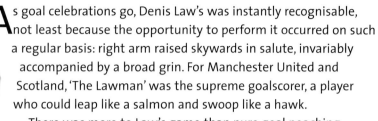

DENIS LAW

GREAT FOOTBALL HEROES

DENIS LAW

Denis Law

Born: Aberdeen, Scotland, 1940

Country: Scotland

International Caps: 55

International Goals: 30

Position: Inside forward

Clubs: Huddersfield, Manchester City, Torino, Manchester United

As goal celebrations go, Denis Law's was instantly recognisable, not least because the opportunity to perform it occurred on such a regular basis: right arm raised skywards in salute, invariably accompanied by a broad grin. For Manchester United and Scotland, 'The Lawman' was the supreme goalscorer, a player who could leap like a salmon and swoop like a hawk.

There was more to Law's game than pure goal poaching, however. He was an astute passer of the ball with the ability to create opportunities for others but it was as a goalscorer, particularly when levering his slim, 5ft 9in frame to rise above taller defenders and power home an unstoppable header, that made him idolised wherever he played.

Coincidentally, Law and his great goalscoring contemporary, Jimmy Greaves, were born within four days of each other. Law hailed from Aberdeen but it was to Huddersfield Town that he went as a teenager in 1955. He made his Scotland debut four years later, scoring in a 3-0 win over Wales. In 1960 he moved to Manchester City for a British record fee of £55,000 and his 21 goals in 44 League appearances at Maine Road encouraged the Italian club Torino to pay a world record fee of £100,000 for him in 1961, including a signing-on fee of £10,000. Despite scoring ten League goals in 27 games in Turin, Law never really settled and was delighted when Matt Busby shelled out yet another record fee (£116,000) to bring him to Old Trafford. Denis Law was now the highest-paid footballer in Britain. Why? Because he was worth it.

He repaid Busby's faith by scoring 23 League goals in his first season plus a Cup Final strike in the victory over Leicester City. Then in 1964 he became only the second British player (after Stanley Matthews) to be named European Footballer of the Year. The holy trinity of Best, Law and Charlton swept United to League titles in 1965 and 1967 on an irresistible tide of attacking football. In those first five seasons Law harvested 160 goals from 222 matches for the club in all competitions. He was often at his best in Europe where he scored no fewer than five hat-tricks although he was bitterly disappointed to miss out on the 1968 European Cup Final because of a knee injury.

Although his habit of playing with his long shirtsleeves gripped in each fist could have been interpreted as a lack of commitment, exactly the opposite was the case. He never gave less than 100 per cent and, as a fierce patriot, was particularly proud to pull on the Scotland shirt. He is the only Scottish player to have scored four goals in a game on two occasions (against Northern Ireland in 1962 and Norway in 1963) and despite appearing in just one World Cup finals tournament (1974), he remains his country's joint top scorer with 30 goals. His lowest point? No contest. England winning the 1966 World Cup! So he took considerable pleasure in being part of the Scotland team that defeated the world champions at Wembley in 1967.

In 1973 Law was controversially given a free transfer by Manchester United boss Tommy Docherty to end an Old Trafford career in which he had scored 236 goals in 393 games. He crossed the city to Maine Road but returned to haunt United the following year. With Docherty's team hurtling towards relegation, Law applied the *coup de grace* in the 85th minute of a crucial end of season encounter with an almost half-hearted back heel that found its way into the United net and consigned them to a 1-0 defeat. Law took no pleasure in seeing his old team relegated. It was one occasion when the famous celebration was utterly subdued and he retired from football immediately after that summer's World Cup.

Having been given a free transfer from Manchester United to Manchester City, Denis Law scored the goal that ensured United's relegation the following year.

TOMMY LAWTON

TOMMY LAWTON

Older Notts County fans still speak in awe of a thunderous header scored by Tommy Lawton against local rivals Nottingham Forest over 50 years ago. Contemporary estimates suggested that the ball travelled anything between 15 and 25 yards and such was its ferocity that the Forest keeper could only flail his arms in surrender as the ball rocketed past him. For Lawton was in that fine tradition of barnstorming English centre forwards who packed a powerful shot but who, above all, were superb in the air.

Born in Bolton, Lawton scored an amazing 570 goals in just three seasons as a schoolboy and joined Second Division Burnley as a sixteen-year-old amateur. He scored twice in his second match and just four days after signing professional forms on his seventeenth birthday, he became the youngest player to score a hat-trick in the Football League when he bagged three goals against Spurs. He quickly became a target for the bigger clubs and on New Year's Eve 1936 he was sold to Everton for £6,500 – a record fee for a teenager. Everton saw him as the natural successor to 'Dixie' Dean and Lawton did not disappoint, finishing top scorer in both 1938 and 1939 (the year Everton won the League Championship) with 28 and 34 League goals apiece. His exploits brought him to the attention of the England selectors who picked him for his first international in 1938. Although England lost 4-2 to Wales at Ninian Park, Cardiff, Lawton marked the occasion by scoring a penalty to become England's youngest-ever goalscorer at nineteen years and seventeen days old.

Hostilities hampered his career over the next six years but he still found time to score 24 goals in 23 wartime internationals while serving as an army physical training instructor. On being demobbed, he elected not to return to Everton but instead signed for Chelsea. Despite setting a new club record with 26 goals in his first season, Lawton was unhappy at the way the club was being run and asked for a transfer. The situation did not harm his international form, however, and in 1946 he became the first England player to score four goals in a game when he helped destroy Holland 8-2.

In 1947 the unsettled Lawton joined Notts County, then in Division Three (South), for a fee of £20,000, making him Britain's most expensive footballer. He won his last England cap in 1949 against Denmark but continued to score freely at club level. His arrival at Meadow Lane had immediately put 10,000 on the gate and he proceeded to score 31 League goals in 37 starts to steer the club to promotion in 1950. After totalling 103 goals in 166 appearances for County, he became player/manager of Brentford in 1952 but struggled to combine the two duties and reverted to being a player only when signing for Arsenal the following year. Scoring thirteen times in 35 matches for the Gunners, he was at least able to bow out at the top. He finally announced his retirement in 1955, having scored a total of 231 League goals in 390 games for his various clubs.

A spell as manager at non-League Kettering Town was followed in 1957 by a return to Meadow Lane in the same capacity. Lawton himself described it as 'a time of my life best forgotten' and was sacked after eleven months in charge. He retired from the game completely to run a public house but was awarded a belated testimonial game at Everton in 1972, which raised more than £6,000. He later became a columnist for the *Nottingham Evening Post*.

Tom Finney reckoned Lawton was the best centre forward he had ever played with. Stanley Matthews was equally unstinting in his praise. 'With Tommy,' said Matthews, 'I could guarantee he would make contact with nine out of ten crosses in the box. He was simply a brilliant header of the ball.' Notts County fans still testify to that.

Tommy Lawton

Born: Bolton, England, 1919 (d. 1996)

Country: England

International Caps: 23

International Goals: 22

Position: Centre forward

Clubs: Burnley, Everton, Chelsea, Notts County, Brentford, Arsenal

Opposite: *Tommy Lawton demonstrating his formidable heading skills in 1947.*

GARY LINEKER

GREAT FOOTBALL HEROES

GARY LINEKER

Gary Lineker. Mr Nice Guy. Once described as the 'Queen Mother of Football'. Never booked, he always seemed to accept whatever the game threw at him with a cheerful smile . . . except when Graham Taylor famously hauled him off against Sweden before he could equal Bobby Charlton's all-time England scoring record. They always say that the most clinical goalscorers need a streak of ruthlessness, nastiness, a desire to humiliate goalkeepers. Lineker was most definitely the exception to the rule.

Yet there were few better penalty area poachers. His timing of runs and his ability to find space were matchless, his finishing economical and precise, always opting for placement rather than power. Shoot low, aim high was Lineker's motto.

The son of a Leicester market trader, Lineker signed for his home town club in 1978 and made his League debut on New Year's Day 1979. He stayed at Filbert Street for seven years, scoring 95 goals in 194 League games, before being transferred to Everton for £1.1 million in 1985 – the year after he made his England debut as a substitute against Scotland. In that first season at Goodison Park he scored 30 League goals, ten more in Cup competitions (including one in the FA Cup Final defeat to Liverpool) and was unsurprisingly named Footballer of the Year.

It was at the 1986 World Cup in Mexico that he really blossomed, scoring six goals in the finals – the highest ever by a British player – to win the Golden Boot award. His hat-trick against Poland (one of five he scored at international level) made him a national hero and also rescued what had hitherto been a dire England campaign.

His value soaring by the minute, he was sold to Terry Venables' Barcelona later in 1986 for £2.75 million and soon became a fans' favourite by scoring all four goals in a game against bitter rivals Real Madrid. He scored an excellent 44 goals in 99 League games for Barcelona, helping them to victories in the Spanish Cup and the European Cup Winners' Cup, which they won in 1989 at the expense of Sampdoria. A few weeks after his European glory he again signed for Venables, this time at Spurs for £1.2 million.

Once again the World Cup brought out the best in him and in 1990 his four goals took England to within one step of the final. His total of ten goals in World Cup finals tournaments is an England record.

Despite finishing First Division top scorer with three different clubs – Leicester, Everton and Spurs – Lineker had yet to add to his Second

Opposite: *Gary Lineker scores against Hungary at Wembley in 1990.*
Below: *His playing days over, Lineker established a new career as a TV presenter.*

Division champions' medal of 1980. This was rectified when Spurs beat Nottingham Forest 2-1 in the 1991 FA Cup Final although Lineker uncharacteristically missed a penalty. Ironically another missed penalty (a casually taken effort in a friendly against Brazil) would ultimately prove costly as it deprived him of the opportunity of equalling Charlton's England total. He spent his last six internationals searching for that elusive goal ... until Graham Taylor put him out of his misery.

After scoring 67 League goals for Spurs in 105 games and being voted Footballer of the Year for a second time, Lineker signed for the Japanese team Grampus Eight. As ever, he was a superb ambassador for his country, learning the language and absorbing the culture, but a persistent toe injury restricted his playing appearances and meant that the Japanese fans never saw him at his sharpest.

It came as no surprise therefore when he announced his retirement from the game in 1994 but soon filled the void with a new media career, fronting *Match of the Day* and becoming a regular team captain on the comedy sports quiz *They Think It's All Over*. He has also starred in TV advertisements where he steals crisps from small boys. No more Mr Nice Guy.

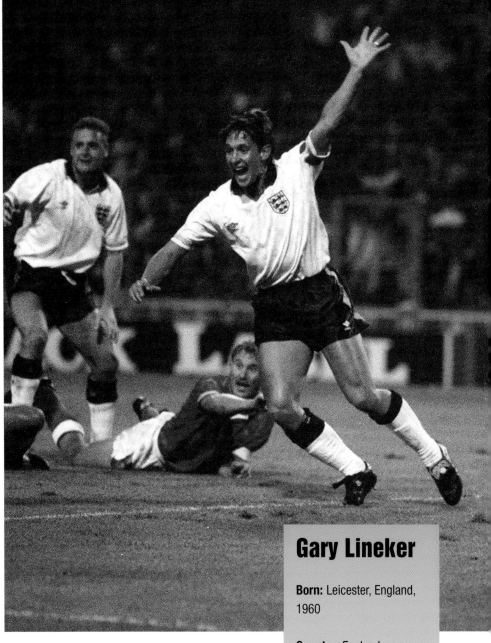

Gary Lineker

Born: Leicester, England, 1960

Country: England

International Caps: 80

International Goals: 48

Position: Striker

Clubs: Leicester, Everton, Barcelona, Tottenham Hotspur, Grampus Eight

DAVE MACKAY

Scotsman Dave Mackay was instrumental in Derby County winning promotion to the English First Division in 1969.

Everyone's favourite photo of Dave Mackay is the one where the barrel-chested Scot, his face contorted in fury, grabs Leeds whippersnapper Billy Bremner by the shirt in reaction to a typical niggling foul. It is reminiscent of a scene from a *Tom and Jerry* cartoon where Spike the bulldog seizes Tom to punish him for some mishap that has befallen his precious pup. The photo is not only cherished because it was Bremner on the receiving end but also because it shows Mackay in all his pomp and majesty, strutting around the pitch.

Every team had its hard man in the sixties, but Mackay was harder – and better – than most. A man of granite, he never shirked a tackle and, although only 5ft 8in tall, his will to win was incredible. One journalist remarked that 'his tackling could have earned him a good living felling trees.' When he broke his left leg, it became the most famous broken leg in football. He even broke the same leg again within the space of a year. Both times surgeons pronounced it to be the end of his career. They didn't know Dave Mackay.

Born in Edinburgh, Mackay joined Hearts in 1952 from the junior side Newtongrange Star and, as a forceful left-half, inspired the Tynecastle club to a Scottish Cup triumph in 1956 and two years later to their first Scottish League title of the century. He also collected two Scottish League Cup winners' medals (1955 and 1959) and was voted Scottish Footballer of the Year in 1958.

In March 1959, two years after winning his first international cap, Mackay headed south to join Bill Nicholson's Tottenham revolution for £30,000. With Mackay and Danny Blanchflower dominating midfield, Spurs swept all before them in 1960-61, surging to a historic League and Cup double. After narrowly losing out on another double the following season, Mackay had the misfortune to miss Spurs' glorious European Cup Winners' Cup Final triumph of 1963, laid low by a severe stomach upset. It must have been one hell of a bug to tangle with Dave Mackay.

If proof were needed of Mackay's importance to Spurs, it was to come in the second leg of their defence of the Cup Winners' Cup against Manchester United at Old Trafford. Leading 2-0 from the first game, Spurs suffered a terrible blow in the early minutes when Mackay broke his left leg while making a typically fearless challenge. Since there was no substitute rule in operation in those days, the Londoners had to battle on with ten men but were unable to hold out, eventually losing 4-1 on the night and 4-3 on aggregate. Courageously Mackay fought his way back to fitness, only to break the leg again in his comeback match for the reserves.

Ignoring the prognosis of the medical experts, he defied the odds and made a complete recovery, topped by captaining Spurs to victory against Chelsea in the 1967 FA Cup Final. The next season was to be his last at Tottenham. 'Spurs were no longer a great side,' he said, 'and frankly I felt I was no longer good enough to be able to do something about it.' After scoring 51 goals in 318 appearances for Spurs, he joined Derby County and immediately led them to promotion to the First Division. In that same year of 1969 he was a popular choice as Footballer of the Year.

In 1971 he moved to Swindon Town as player/manager before hanging up his boots. He had various spells in management but his most successful by far was at Derby where he replaced Brian Clough in 1974 and within a year had taken the Rams to the League Championship.

Managers may come and go but when it comes to discussing hard men Dave Mackay was in a class of his own. He could have eaten Vinnie Jones for breakfast.

Dave Mackay

Born: Edinburgh, Scotland, 1934

Country: Scotland

International Caps: 22

International Goals: 4

Position: Midfield/Defence

Clubs: Hearts, Tottenham Hotspur, Derby County, Swindon Town

GREAT FOOTBALL HEROES

PAOLO MALDINI

Opposite: *Paolo Maldini
starred for AC Milan, following
in the footsteps of his father,
who captained the club.*

Paolo Maldini

Born: Milan, Italy, 1968

Country: Italy

International Caps: 126

International Goals: 7

Position: Defence

Clubs: AC Milan

PAOLO MALDINI

The face that launched a thousand posters, Paolo Maldini has been a stalwart of the AC Milan defence for eighteen years. In that time he has played over 600 games for the club and won a record 126 caps for his country, becoming a favourite with sports fans and teenage girls alike.

Tall, blue-eyed and dashingly handsome, Maldini has long been a media darling. Fashion mogul Giorgio Armani once said he would love to use him as a model. On the football pitch Maldini has been just about the best left-back in the world, composed under pressure and clean in the tackle. Comfortable on the ball, he is also dangerous going forward, offering a regular outlet for attacking moves down the left flank. But above all he exudes style, class and confidence. Even a wayward back-pass looks entirely intentional if it is made by Paolo Maldini.

Sons of famous footballing fathers have a lot to live up to – just ask Darren Ferguson, Jordi Cruyff or Paul Dalglish – but Maldini has remained unfazed by any comparisons with father Cesare, a former captain of Milan and manager of Italy. Although Cesare played for Milan and Paolo was born in the city, Maldini junior was a fan of Juventus in his youth, his hero being Roberto Bettega. However, when it came to a career he chose to join Milan's youth system under the coaching direction of his father. At first he played on the left wing but then decided to switch to defence – the same position where Cesare Maldini had performed with such distinction. For many it would have been a daunting prospect but young Maldini coped admirably with the inevitable attention and made his Serie A debut at the age of sixteen in January 1985, coming on as a substitute during a 1-1 draw away to Udinese.

He would soon make the left-back spot his own although in recent years he has also played at centre-half for Milan. With Milan he has won six League titles and three European Cups – against Steaua Bucharest in 1989, Benfica in 1990 and Barcelona in 1994. He was also part of the Milan team that remained unbeaten for 58 League matches spanning a period of seventeen months until Parma ended their run in March 1993. The following year Maldini's achievements were recognised when he was named World Player of the Year.

He made his international debut in 1988 against Yugoslavia and has played in four World Cup finals tournaments, taking over as captain from Franco Baresi in 1995. Although his international career has been a record-breaking affair, it is tinged with sadness for Maldini as Italy have so often narrowly missed out on winning the major tournaments. Italia '90 was a case in point. Italy had yet to concede a goal before the semi-final with Argentina and, on home soil, started the match as warm favourites, only to lose in a penalty shoot-out – the downfall of many an Italian team over the years. Euro 2000 was even worse, victory in the final snatched from Italy's grasp by France in the dying seconds of normal time before David Trezeguet's Golden Goal winner. Maldini admitted afterwards: 'I keep on thinking about those final 30 seconds and the hundred different ways we could have handled things and become European champions.'

However his toughest period at international level was when his father was appointed coach of Italy in 1996 and later sacked following a disappointing showing at the 1998 World Cup. 'My mother aged ten years during that period,' said Paolo. 'In a dressing-room, it's normal for players to jeer the coach and poke fun at him but as soon as I would walk in, the lads would change the subject. My father was very disappointed when he was sacked. So too was I.'

Even Paolo Maldini's life hasn't always been perfect.

Diego Maradona

Born: Buenos Aires, Argentina, 1960

Country: Argentina

International Caps: 91

International Goals: 34

Position: Midfield/Striker

Clubs: Argentinos Juniors, Boca Juniors, Barcelona, Napoli, Seville

GREAT FOOTBALL HEROES

MARADONA

DIEGO MARADONA

Before the 1986 World Cup quarter-final against Argentina, England manager Bobby Robson warned journalists of the greatest threat awaiting his team. 'Maradona,' he said, 'can win a game on his own in five minutes.' How prophetic those words would turn out to be. For no sooner had Maradona given Argentina the lead with his infamous 'Hand of God' goal, punching the ball into the net over the advancing Peter Shilton, than he followed it up with a second, picking the ball up inside his own half and waltzing past five defenders and Shilton to score a goal that was as sublime as the first had been unjust.

That quick-fire double somehow encapsulated his career – capable of sheer brilliance but also more than capable of cheating. His subsequent brushes with authority have meant that Diego Maradona is remembered as much for failing drugs tests as for his wizardry on the pitch.

He was always an unlikely superstar. Short, stocky and almost solely reliant on his left foot, at first glance he would have struggled to make a parks side. But with the ball at his feet he was poetry in motion, boasting devastating acceleration, immaculate control and balance, and considerable body strength that made it so difficult for defenders to knock him off the ball. He was like a pocket battleship and at his best was the most exciting player in the world.

He made his League debut as a fifteen-year-old for Argentinos Juniors in 1976 and earned his first international call-up the following year, only to fall out with national coach Cesar Menotti after being left out of the squad for the 1978 World Cup. Reconciled with Menotti, he starred in the 1979 World Youth Cup in Japan before moving to Boca Juniors for £1 million, a record fee for a teenager. Although his ugly side surfaced in the 1982 World Cup when he was sent off for a terrible tackle, his undisputed talent persuaded Barcelona to pay a world record £4.2 million to secure his signature. He suffered a torrid time in Spain, being put out of the game for four months by a reckless tackle from Bilbao hatchet man Andoni Goicoechea, and in 1984 was transferred to Italian side Napoli for a third world record fee of £5 million. Napoli president Corrado Ferlaino had struggled to raise the money but was repaid within weeks as the club sold a staggering 70,000 season tickets on the back of Maradona's signing.

By captaining Argentina to victory at the 1986 World Cup (he repeated his magical England goal against Belgium), he was unanimously voted Player of the Tournament and acclaimed a national hero. He was almost as popular in Italy where, in 1987, he led Napoli to a long-awaited League title as well as the Italian Cup. By the time he had helped his team win the UEFA Cup in 1989, Neapolitan salesmen were doing a roaring trade in Maradona wigs!

But his love affair with Italian football turned sour in the semi-final of the 1990 World Cup when Argentina defeated the hosts on penalties in Maradona's adopted home of Naples, a result which saw some Italian fans turn on him. Worse was to follow in 1991 when he failed a drugs test and was given a fifteen-month ban. He returned to Argentina where he was arrested for possession of cocaine. Released on probation, he tried to resurrect his career with the Spanish side Seville but his temperamental ways led to him being sacked after barely half a season.

Back in Argentina he made another playing comeback with his old love Boca Juniors and worked his way into the Argentina team for the 1994 World Cup. This produced his greatest humiliation of all when he was sent home from the tournament for failing another drugs test. After yet more attempted comebacks, Maradona finally retired in 1997, an outstanding talent ultimately destroyed by his own personal demons.

Diego Maradona after captaining Argentina to victory in the 1986 World Cup final in Mexico, beating West Germany 3-2.

LOTHAR MATTHÄUS

LOTHAR MATTHÄUS

When it comes to endurance records, nobody can match combative German midfielder Lothar Matthäus. He has won more international caps than any other player in the world, has appeared in a record 25 matches at the World Cup finals and is one of only two players (the other being Mexican goalkeeper Antonio Carbajal) to have appeared in five World Cup tournaments. His supreme self-confidence and outspoken nature have not always endeared him to team-mates or coaches but nobody can deny that he has been a player of the highest calibre.

Born in Erlangen, he began his career with a local club called FC Herzogenaurach, combining playing with his studies for interior design. In 1979 he decided to take the plunge and turn professional with Borussia Mönchengladbach, then one of the most powerful clubs in Europe. He scored for Borussia in their 1980 UEFA Cup Final defeat to Eintracht Frankfurt and in the same year made his debut for the national side as a substitute against Holland at the European Championships. Two years later he made his first World Cup appearance, coming on as substitute in the 4-1 victory over Chile.

In 1984 he moved to Bayern Munich for a German record fee of £650,000. In four years with Bayern he scored 57 goals in 117 League games, driving them to three consecutive Bundesliga titles from 1985-87 and two German Cups. At the 1986 World Cup Matthäus scored the winner against Morocco in the second round and went on to play in the final where, despite suffering from a broken wrist, he was given a man-marking job on Maradona. However the little Argentinian had too many tricks up his sleeve and the Germans lost 3-2, Maradona providing the pass for the winning goal.

By the time the World Cup was held in Italy in 1990, Matthäus was an established star with Inter Milan whom he had joined in 1988 for £2.4 million and had led to the Serie A title a year later. As captain and midfield general, he was the heartbeat of the German team. Any move of note seemed to originate from his feet and he also found time to surge forward and score four goals in the course of the tournament. Once again the Germans faced Argentina in the final but this time Maradona had to play second fiddle. As well as being a World Cup winner, Matthäus was voted Player of the Tournament, European Footballer of the Year and World Footballer of the Year.

His penalty in the first leg of the 1991 UEFA Cup Final helped Inter

Lothar Matthäus

Born: Erlangen, Germany, 1961

Country: Germany

International Caps: 150

International Goals: 23

Position: Midfield/ Defence

Clubs: Borussia Mönchengladbach, Bayern Munich, Inter Milan, Metrostars

Milan to aggregate victory over Italian rivals Roma but after missing the 1992 European Championships with a knee injury, he returned to Germany and Bayern. His second spell at the club lasted eight years, in which time he guided them to two more Bundesliga titles (in 1994 and 1997) and a UEFA Cup victory in 1996. When Bayern sensationally lost to Manchester United in the dying seconds of the 1999 European Cup Final, Matthäus decided that it was time to be on his way and shortly afterwards he travelled to the United States to sign for the New Jersey-based Metrostars.

Lothar Matthäus in 1996 during his second period with Bayern Munich.

The serious knee injury from 1992 had left his international career under a cloud but he regained his place the following year and was a key member of Germany's team at the 1994 World Cup where he dropped back from midfield to sweeper, a role calculated to accommodate his experience and ageing legs. He scored once but Germany crashed out to Bulgaria in the quarter-finals. That was expected to be his international curtain call but, at the age of 37, he was surprisingly selected for France '98 as a replacement for the injured Mattias Sammer and when he came on as a substitute against Yugoslavia he set that new World Cup appearances record.

STANLEY MATTHEWS

STANLEY MATTHEWS

It was every full-back's worst nightmare. Stanley Matthews was standing five yards away with the ball at his feet. Opponents knew what was coming but such was Matthews' balance and dexterity that invariably they were unable to prevent it. A moment's hesitation or an ill-timed lunge and he would suddenly sway in the opposite direction and dart off to the by-line before delivering one of those trademark pinpoint crosses. His old England centre forward Tommy Lawton used to joke that Matthews could regularly put the ball on his centre-parting. It was no exaggeration.

And that was Matthews' game, teasing and tormenting full-backs, laying on goals for others. 'Stan was unique,' said Joe Mercer. 'He never went for 50-50 balls, didn't score many goals, and was not good in the air. But on his day he was unplayable. He beat fellows so easily, with such pace and balance, often taking on four or five at a time.' From 1932 when he made his League debut with his local club, Stoke City, until 1965 when he finally retired from top-flight football at the ripe old age of 50, Stanley Matthews was arguably the most popular player in Britain.

The 'Wizard of the Dribble', as he became known, owed his longevity in the game to strict discipline. He never drank or smoked, regularly ate salads and always got up before six in the morning to exercise.

He started out with Stoke on £1 a week and in his first spell at the Victoria Ground scored 51 goals in 259 League appearances. When he fell out with the manager in 1938 and asked for a transfer, the sense of apprehension in the Potteries was such that businessmen claimed factory production was being adversely affected. Following a mass protest meeting, the dispute was finally settled amicably. Normal service was resumed, both on and off the pitch.

He had made his England debut against Wales in 1935 but went on to win only 54 caps as the FA selectors struggled to accommodate him in their line-up. His repeated omission was deemed a national disgrace.

At 32, Stoke probably thought Matthews was over the hill and so they sold him to Blackpool for £11,500. It was a mistake. The following season he won the inaugural Footballer of the Year award and helped Blackpool to reach three FA Cup Finals in the space of five years. Following two Wembley defeats, all neutrals were hoping it would be third time lucky for Matthews in the 1953 final against Bolton Wanderers. Things looked bleak as Blackpool trailed 3-1 with 20 minutes remaining but the inspirational Matthews helped haul them back to 3-3 before laying on the winner for Bill Perry in the last minute. Although Stan Mortensen scored a hat-trick for Blackpool, the match has gone down in history as 'The Matthews Final'.

The first European Footballer of the Year in 1956, he made his last international appearance the following year but was still going strong in League football. After 379 League outings for Blackpool (seventeen goals), he rejoined Stoke in 1961. Signing a 46-year-old was considered a gimmick but Matthews put 27,000 on the gate and helped Stoke to promotion to the First Division. He was again named Footballer of the Year in 1963 and even at the age of 48, played in 35 of Stoke's matches that season. His final game was against Fulham in February 1965 – five days after his 50th birthday. He remains the only man over 50 to have played top-flight football in England.

To mark his retirement he was awarded a knighthood (the first professional footballer to receive such an honour) and world stars such as Di Stefano, Puskas and Yashin turned out for his testimonial game. After three years as general manager at Port Vale, he disappeared from football and went to live in Malta. His death in 2000 was met with fulsome tributes in recognition of a remarkable talent.

Stanley Matthews

Born: Stoke, England, 1915 (d. 2000)

Country: England

International Caps: 54

International Goals: 11

Position: Right wing

Clubs: Stoke City, Blackpool

Opposite: *Stanley Matthews in England colours, aged 38.*
Below: *Laying on the winning goal in 'The Matthews Final'.*

Guiseppe Meazza

Born: Milan, Italy, 1910 (d. 1979)

Country: Italy

International Caps: 53

International Goals: 33

Position: Centre forward

Clubs: Inter Milan, AC Milan, Juventus, Atalanta

GUISEPPE MEAZZA

Guiseppe Meazza was Italian football's first superstar. Nicknamed 'Peppino', he was a graceful centre forward with never a single Brylcreemed hair out of place. The highlights of his career were two World Cup triumphs – the second as Italy's captain.

Born in Milan, he made his debut with Inter at the age of seventeen, marking his arrival by scoring twice in a Cup game. In his second season he set a new club record with 33 goals (twice netting five in a game and once, against Venezia, scoring six). In 1930 he was the League's top goalscorer – a feat he would repeat on two more occasions (1936 and 1938). He was particularly deadly in one-on-one situations, delighting in rounding the keeper before stroking the ball into the net. In 1933 Juventus and Italy keeper Giampiero Combi had the temerity to suggest that Meazza would not be able to sidestep him. Meazza told his friend to put his money where his mouth was and Combi duly accepted the bet. When Inter and Juventus next met, Meazza set off on a dazzling run from the half-way line, leaving several defenders trailing in his wake, before dummying Combi and scoring. Combi went straight up to him and shook his hand. With Meazza such a consistent marksman, Inter won the Serie A title in 1930 and 1938 and the Coppa Italia in 1939.

He made his international debut against Switzerland in 1930, scoring twice, and went one better three months later with a hat-trick against Hungary. He remained a virtual ever-present in the national side for nine years, Vittorio Pozzo, the Italy coach, having taken the decision to switch Meazza from his club position of centre forward to an inside-forward berth that would allow him to use his passing skills to better effect.

In 1934 Meazza was one of only a handful of home-grown talents in the Italian World Cup team, the remainder being South Americans. When quizzed about this, Pozzo said that if the South Americans could die for Italy (they were eligible for national service), they could play football for the country, and FIFA chose to turn a blind eye. Inspired by Meazza, who scored two goals in the tournament including a

GREAT FOOTBALL HEROES

GUISEPPE MEAZZA

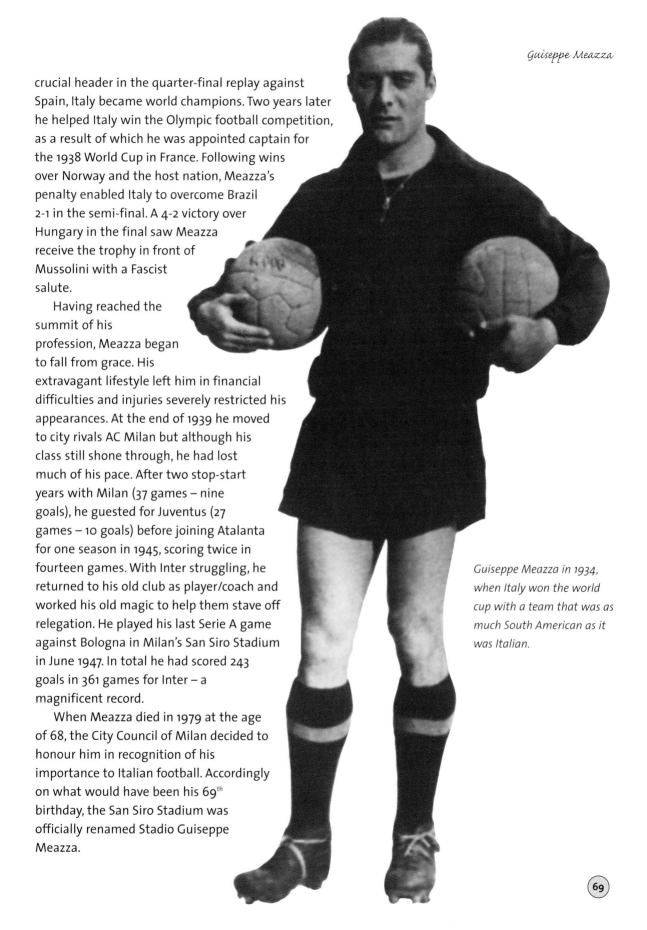

crucial header in the quarter-final replay against Spain, Italy became world champions. Two years later he helped Italy win the Olympic football competition, as a result of which he was appointed captain for the 1938 World Cup in France. Following wins over Norway and the host nation, Meazza's penalty enabled Italy to overcome Brazil 2-1 in the semi-final. A 4-2 victory over Hungary in the final saw Meazza receive the trophy in front of Mussolini with a Fascist salute.

Having reached the summit of his profession, Meazza began to fall from grace. His extravagant lifestyle left him in financial difficulties and injuries severely restricted his appearances. At the end of 1939 he moved to city rivals AC Milan but although his class still shone through, he had lost much of his pace. After two stop-start years with Milan (37 games – nine goals), he guested for Juventus (27 games – 10 goals) before joining Atalanta for one season in 1945, scoring twice in fourteen games. With Inter struggling, he returned to his old club as player/coach and worked his old magic to help them stave off relegation. He played his last Serie A game against Bologna in Milan's San Siro Stadium in June 1947. In total he had scored 243 goals in 361 games for Inter – a magnificent record.

When Meazza died in 1979 at the age of 68, the City Council of Milan decided to honour him in recognition of his importance to Italian football. Accordingly on what would have been his 69th birthday, the San Siro Stadium was officially renamed Stadio Guiseppe Meazza.

Guiseppe Meazza in 1934, when Italy won the world cup with a team that was as much South American as it was Italian.

Roger Milla

Born: Yaoundé, Cameroon, 1952

Country: Cameroon

International Caps: 81

International Goals: 42

Position: Centre forward

Clubs: Éclair de Douala, Léopard de Douala, Tonnerre Yaoundé, Valenciennes, AS Monaco, Bastia, Saint Etienne, Montpellier

GREAT FOOTBALL HEROES

ROGER MILLA

ROGER MILLA

Roger Milla is the grand old man of the World Cup. He first exploded onto the scene in the 1990 finals at the age of 38 and was tempted out of retirement for a second time four years later where, at 42, he became the oldest goalscorer in the history of the tournament. At an age when some men haven't seen their feet for years, Milla was still wiggling his hips around the corner flag in that famous goal celebration.

Milla was born in the Cameroon capital of Yaoundé but his father's job on the railways meant that the family was often on the move. Wherever he ended up, the football-mad youngster found somewhere to play barefoot and soon earned himself the nickname 'Pele'. He signed for his first club, Éclair de Douala, when he was 13 and even at that tender age displayed remarkable technique as well as an eye for goal. In 1970 he joined Léopard de Douala with whom he won the Cameroon Championship before moving to Tonnerre Yaoundé. People began to sit up and take notice of the emerging talent in 1976 when Milla's goals helped Tonnerre win the African Cup Winners' Cup. In the same year he made his international debut, was named African Footballer of the Year and achieved what he hoped would be his dream move to Europe with French club Valenciennes. To Milla's great frustration he spent most of his two years languishing in the reserves. He fared little better with AS Monaco, either sitting on the bench or in the treatment room, nor with the Corsican club Bastia, but a move to Saint Etienne in 1984 helped him rediscover his goal touch. He scored 22 goals in 31 appearances there before another transfer took him to Montpellier. He finally retired from French club football in 1989 with 152 goals to his name.

With most football stories that would be the end, but with Milla it was just the beginning. He had already appeared in the 1982 World Cup finals – Cameroon's first – where the Lions were unlucky to be eliminated on goal difference in a group that included Poland, Peru and Italy. Two years later he was top scorer with four goals as Cameroon won the African Cup of Nations and in 1986 he was voted Player of the Tournament in the same competition. Then in 1987 he announced his retirement from international football and, after testimonials at Douala and Yaoundé that drew nearly 100,000 fans, he moved to Reunion Island in the Pacific for what he thought would be a quiet retirement. His peace was shattered by a phone call from the President of Cameroon, begging him to come out of retirement in his country's hour of need. Milla could not refuse such a plea and so it was that his electric bursts of pace and mesmerising runs came to light up Italia '90, scoring four goals as Cameroon exceeded all expectations to reach the quarter-finals – the first African nation to reach that round. It took two Gary Lineker penalties to see them off. To mark his achievements, Milla was again named African Player of the Year, the first man to win the award twice.

Once more Milla announced his retirement, only to be tempted back for the 1994 World Cup. Although Cameroon were eliminated at the group stage, Milla's historic consolation goal against Russia was one of the most popular moments of the entire event. This time he retired for good, the first African to have played in three World Cup finals tournaments.

There have been more gifted footballers down the years but Roger Milla's middle-aged exploits made him a national hero, a role model for thousands of African children. And that counts for a lot.

Roger Milla shoots past England's Paul Parker during the 1990 World Cup quarter-final match.

BOBBY MOORE

Opposite left: *Bobby Moore was a popular choice to appear on commemorative stamps.*
Opposite right: *England's World Cup captain, 1966.*

Bobby Moore

Born: London, England, 1941 (d. 1993)

Country: England

International Caps: 108

International Goals: 2

Position: Defence

Clubs: West Ham, Fulham

BOBBY MOORE

'Bobby Moore was my captain, my leader, my right-hand man. He was the spirit and the heartbeat of the team, a cool, calculating footballer I could trust with my life. He was the supreme professional, the best I ever worked with. Without him England would never have won the World Cup.' Those were the words of Sir Alf Ramsey, the man who, in 1963, had made the 22-year-old Moore England's youngest-ever captain. Ramsey was a man rarely given to idle flattery. Praise from him was praise indeed. But the remark is a measure of the esteem in which Moore was held not only by the England manager but also by the English public. For when Moore climbed the steps to the Royal Box to receive the Jules Rimet Trophy, pausing only to wipe his hands on the velvet drapes before greeting the Queen, he was more than just a footballer, he symbolised the joy of the nation. He was England's Golden Boy, someone with a knack for saying and doing the right thing. At that moment he was almost royalty himself.

In some respects he had come a long way from his Barking roots but in others he hadn't travelled very far at all. He still played for his local team, West Ham, whom he had led to FA Cup success in 1964, followed by a European Cup Winners' Cup triumph the following year. Despite these glories – and the accolade of being named Footballer of the Year in 1964 – he remained essentially an East End boy. He had first joined the Hammers in 1958 and remained with the club for sixteen years, but was denied the League title he craved and which his performances surely warranted. While West Ham were great entertainers, they had a soft underbelly.

The same could not be said of Moore. Although he invariably looked the picture of innocence, he was uncompromising and hard in the tackle. Another anomaly was that for one who played at left-half his right foot was the stronger. Nor was he blessed with a defender's natural pace but relied almost solely on timing, perfectly illustrated by that exquisite tackle against Brazil in the 1970 World Cup – an incident shown almost as regularly as Banks' save from Pele.

That World Cup was a traumatic affair for Moore who, before the tournament began, had been accused of stealing a bracelet from a Bogota jeweller's shop. Following the intervention of the FA and the Foreign Office, he was eventually released without charge and it is a mark of his professionalism that, straight after his ordeal, he was able to play to such a high standard against the best players in the world.

Back in England he grew restless, however, and sought a move to a bigger club. Instead, in 1974, he joined Fulham, then a retirement home for ageing footballers. After 544 League games for the Hammers, he played another 124 with Fulham for whom he also appeared in the 1975 FA Cup Final, only to finish on the losing side . . . to West Ham. He had played his last international in 1974, having worn the captain's armband on 90 occasions (thereby equalling Billy Wright's England record), and duly retired from League football in 1977. He tried his luck at management with Southend United but never came close to emulating his achievements as a player and drifted into the twilight world of match summarising on radio.

When Moore died of cancer in 1993 at the age of 51, his old adversary Pele led the tributes. 'The world has lost one of its greatest players,' he said, 'and a great gentleman.' Many people who had never even met him felt the poorer for his passing. That was the effect Bobby Moore had on us all.

GERD MÜLLER

GERD MÜLLER

In 1964 Bayern Munich president Wilhelm Neudecker oversaw the signing of a promising young striker from TSV Nordlingen by the name of Gerd Müller. But the Bayern coach, Tschik Cajkovski, took one look at the new boy and sniffed: 'I can't put that little elephant in among my string of thoroughbreds.' Müller went on to spend almost sixteen years at Bayern, during which time he scored 365 goals in 427 League matches, helped his team to four Bundesliga titles and a hat-trick of European Cup successes. He also scored the goal that won the World Cup for West Germany in 1974.

In fairness to Cajkovski, Müller did not exactly look like someone who would turn into the most feared penalty box predator of his day. He was short and heavy with thighs that were as thick as tree trunks but his strength and low centre of gravity made him a real handful in the box where he could wriggle and dart free from his mountainous markers to find that precious yard of space so essential to all great goalscorers. He could turn on a sixpence and his reflexes were razor sharp with the result that 'Der Bomber', as he became known, rarely wasted an opportunity within eighteen yards of goal. Like Jimmy Greaves, he rarely bothered shooting from distance or picking the ball up in deep positions; all his work was done where it mattered. Yet whilst the vast majority of his goals were close range efforts, there was tremendous variety in his execution – bicycle kicks, diving headers, thundering volleys or simple tap-ins. They all came the same to Gerd Müller.

Although raised in a small village that had no football ground, Müller was always determined to make the grade and even as a youngster practised for hours on end, sharpening the skills that would stand him in good stead in years to come. These attributes brought him to the notice of Nordlingen who signed him in 1962 as a seventeen-year-old. Two years later and he was off to Bayern where in 1966 he helped his new club secure the German Cup. He made his international debut that year in a 2-0 win over Turkey, but it was the following season that he really began to make a name for himself. His 28 goals made him top scorer in the Bundesliga – a feat he was to repeat in 1968, 1970, 1972, 1973, 1974 (jointly) and 1978 – and he helped Bayern win the European Cup Winners' Cup with an extra-time victory over Glasgow Rangers in Nuremberg. As a result he was voted Germany's Footballer of the Year.

By the 1970 World Cup, the Germans had the luxury of two top-class

Gerd Müller

Born: Nordlingen, Germany, 1945

Country: Germany

International Caps: 62

International Goals: 68

Position: Centre forward

Clubs: TSV Nordlingen, Bayern Munich

but similar strikers in Müller and the veteran Uwe Seeler. Rather than have them competing for the same spot, the coach moved Seeler back into midfield. Both players scored in the quarter-final victory over England, Müller going on to finish top scorer in the tournament with ten goals, including a hat-trick against Bulgaria and two in the heartbreaking semi-final defeat to Italy. Accordingly he was named European Footballer of the Year – the first German to win the award.

His stock increased with a match-winning brace in the final of the 1972 European Championships against the USSR and four more goals at the 1974 World Cup, among them a late semi-final winner to see off Poland and then the dramatic strike that lifted the trophy itself at the expense of Holland. His total of fourteen goals in World Cup finals matches remains a record. But he wasn't finished yet and in 1976 netted against Czechoslovakia in the final of the European Championships to become the first player to score in two finals of that competition. He retired from playing in 1981 with a career total of 628 goals in first-class football. Not bad for a 'little elephant'.

Peter Bonetti looks on in vain as Gerd Müller scores against England during the 1970 World Cup. Germany won 3-2 after being 2-0 down.

Daniel Passarella

Born: Buenos Aires, Argentina, 1953

Country: Argentina

International Caps: 70

International Goals: 22

Position: Defence

Clubs: Sarmiento, River Plate, Fiorentina, Inter Milan

Opposite: *Daniel Passarella, captain of Argentina, raises the trophy as he is carried shoulder high by fans after Argentina beat Holland 3-1 in the 1978 World Cup final.*

GREAT FOOTBALL HEROES

DANIEL PASSARELLA

DANIEL PASSARELLA

Unfortunately Daniel Passarella's outstanding player career has tended to be overshadowed by some of his bizarre edicts as a manager. For the man who was a commanding centre half for clubs at home and in Italy and who lifted the World Cup in 1978 as captain of Argentina made all the wrong sorts of headlines on taking over as coach of his country in 1994. Although Passarella himself had worn his hair long in his playing days, he decreed that in future he would not be selecting any players with flowing locks. To show that he wasn't solely blinkered by the hair issue, he also banned homosexuals and players with earrings. Argentina were thus faced with the prospect of taking a squad of about five to the 1998 World Cup.

Fernando Redondo of Real Madrid was so appalled by the rulings that he flatly refused to join the squad and even ace goalscorer Gabriel Batistuta – the man they call 'Batigol' – was only permitted to play after making an enforced visit to the barber's. Argentine football had become a laughing stock.

Yet as a player Passarella had been a national hero, a leader of men who enjoyed the unqualified support of his team-mates. And he led by example. He was comfortable with the ball at his feet if playing as a sweeper and, although only 5ft 10in tall, was dominant in the air when operating more as an old-fashioned centre half. His heading was undoubtedly his strongpoint, whether clearing his own lines or threatening the opposition goal at corners and free-kicks. For a defender his scoring record was second to none, boasting over 150 goals in senior football.

After starting his career with Sarmiento of Argentina in 1971, Passarella moved to River Plate three years later, making his debut for them in a 1-0 defeat to Rosario Central. It was a rare setback as he went on to captain River Plate to four Argentinian League titles in the 1970s.

He made his first international appearance at the age of 23 but rapidly rose to captain in time for the 1978 World Cup. This was Passarella's finest hour in the famous blue and white stripes, his inspirational leadership and determined defending providing the solid platform from which the likes of Mario Kempes were able to wreak havoc in the opposition penalty area. Although there were dark mutterings about the performance of Peru's Argentinian-born goalkeeper Ramon Quiroga in the deciding second round group match (the hitherto impressive Peru suddenly capitulated 6-0 to allow the hosts through at the expense of Brazil), Argentina emerged as worthy

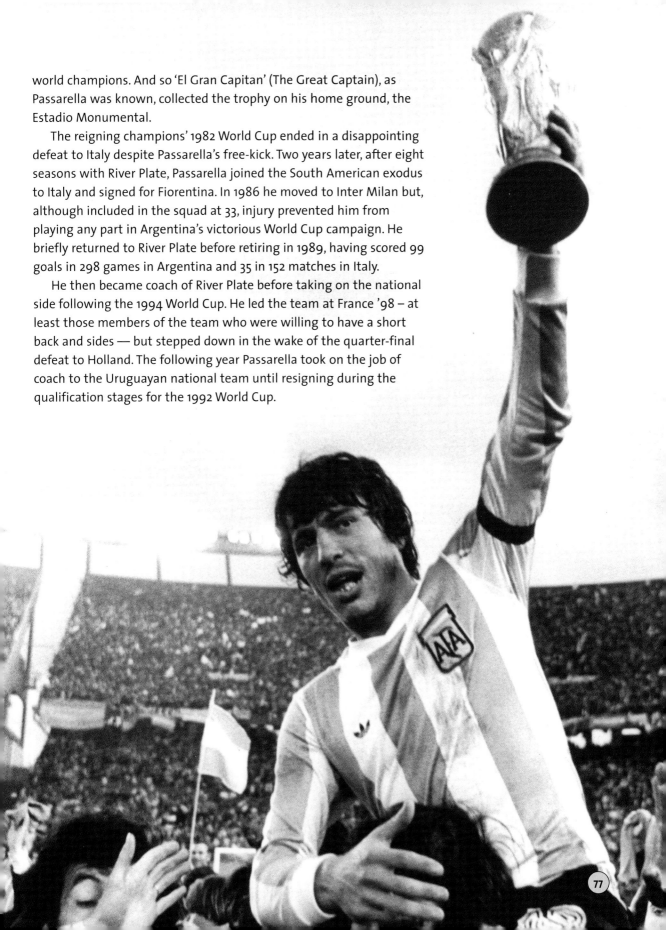

world champions. And so 'El Gran Capitan' (The Great Captain), as Passarella was known, collected the trophy on his home ground, the Estadio Monumental.

The reigning champions' 1982 World Cup ended in a disappointing defeat to Italy despite Passarella's free-kick. Two years later, after eight seasons with River Plate, Passarella joined the South American exodus to Italy and signed for Fiorentina. In 1986 he moved to Inter Milan but, although included in the squad at 33, injury prevented him from playing any part in Argentina's victorious World Cup campaign. He briefly returned to River Plate before retiring in 1989, having scored 99 goals in 298 games in Argentina and 35 in 152 matches in Italy.

He then became coach of River Plate before taking on the national side following the 1994 World Cup. He led the team at France '98 – at least those members of the team who were willing to have a short back and sides — but stepped down in the wake of the quarter-final defeat to Holland. The following year Passarella took on the job of coach to the Uruguayan national team until resigning during the qualification stages for the 1992 World Cup.

GREAT FOOTBALL HEROES

PELE

Pele

Born: Tres Coracoes, Brazil, 1940

Country: Brazil

International Caps: 92

International Goals: 77

Position: Inside forward

Clubs: Bauru, Santos, New York Cosmos

PELE

In 1958 South America's best-kept secret was unleashed upon the rest of the world. A lithe, agile seventeen-year-old burst into the World Cup, scoring a hat-trick for Brazil against France in the semi-final and following up with two more goals in the final against Sweden. Brazil were world champions and Edson Arantes do Nascimento was the talk of the town. The world would come to know him as Pele.

Almost every poll of the world's greatest-ever footballers puts Pele at the top. A staggering career total of 1,283 goals in 1,363 first-class matches, three times a World Cup winner, perpetrator of outrageous dummies on goalkeepers and shots from the half-way line, it's a no-contest. It wasn't just what Pele did, but how he did it. He had magical passing and dribbling skills, breathtaking ball control, he had pace, he had strength and he was a deadly finisher. And he did it all with such grace and rhythm, playing football to a samba beat.

Born in Tres Coracoes, Pele spent an impoverished childhood in southern Brazil where he enjoyed the basics of soccer from an early age, often playing with a ball made out of old socks. His father, Dondhino, was a moderate centre forward with a minor league club and encouraged the boy's interest in the game but his mother wanted something better for him. Pele was determined to step into his father's boots and dropped out of school at the age of nine to pursue his dream of becoming a professional footballer. While his father coached him in soccer, young Pele earned money as a cobbler's apprentice.

Pele's precocious skill came to the attention of former Brazilian international Waldemar de Brito who encouraged him to join Bauru, a club based in Sao Paulo. Then, in 1956, Pele moved to Santos and over the next eighteen years he would help them win nine Brazilian Championships. He made his first League appearance at fifteen and in 1957 scored on his international debut against Argentina. But it was the 1958 World Cup that thrust him into the limelight, notably a brilliant goal in the final where he trapped a ball on his thigh in a packed penalty area, hooked it over his head, whirled round and volleyed it past the startled Swedish keeper.

He missed the 1962 World Cup Final after tearing a thigh muscle in the second match of the tournament and in 1966 the butchers of Portugal kicked him all over Goodison Park. Fortunately for lovers of the beautiful game, he was still around for 1970 even though, in the wake of his experiences in England, he had originally vowed never to play in another World Cup. The 1970 Brazil team was filled to the brim with flamboyant players but Pele stood head and shoulders above them all. Having scored three goals *en route* to the final, he saved his best until last, scoring one (a powerful header) and laying on two more as Italy were crushed 4-1. It was a fitting swansong as shortly afterwards he retired from international football.

He played on with Santos for another four years (his 1,000[th] goal had been a penalty against Vasco da Gama in 1969) before deciding to retire at 34. Santos marked his passing by removing the famous No. 10 shirt from their line-up. It was an admission that nobody could compare with Pele.

In 1975 he came out of retirement to play for New York Cosmos, staying for two years before adopting a role as a sporting ambassador. In 1994 he was appointed Brazil's Minister for Sport and was later named Athlete of the Century.

Pele once said: 'I was born for soccer, just as Beethoven was born for music.' In other mouths this would have sounded arrogant; in Pele's it was merely a statement of fact.

Pele accelerates past a Swedish defender during an international match in 1960. In 1999, the International Olympic Committee named Pele as one of the five Sportsmen of the Century alongside Muhammad Ali, Carl Lewis, Michael Jordan, and Mark Spitz.

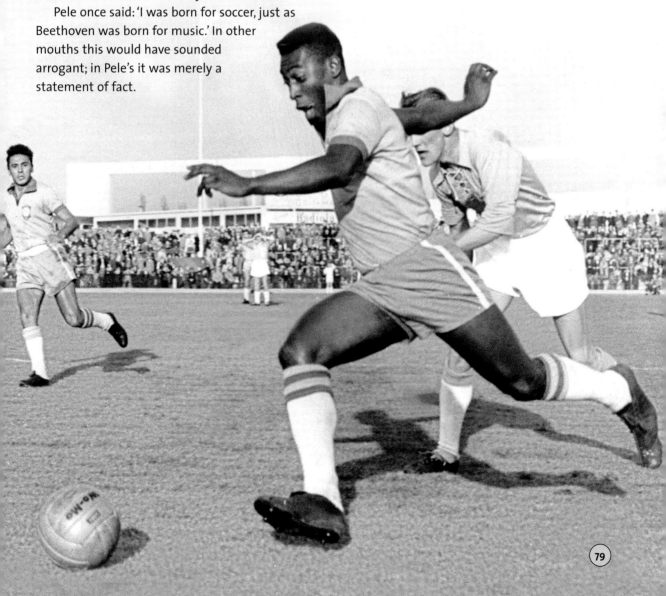

MICHEL PLATINI

MICHEL PLATINI

Michel Platini put France on the footballing map in the 1980s. An elegant midfielder with an eye for goal, he stamped his class on those around him and became his country's number one sports personality. At the end of a distinguished career, just about the only honour missing was a World Cup winners' medal. In that respect, too, Platini was ahead of his time.

It was a career that began in the small town of Joeuf in the east of France. The grandson of an Italian immigrant, Platini played for the local team as a youngster but in 1972 joined AS Nancy-Lorraine where his father was coach. As his talents reached a wider audience, he would go on to play for Saint Etienne and eventually Juventus. He was fond of remarking: 'I began by playing for the biggest club in the Lorraine region, went on to the biggest club in France and ended up with the biggest in the world.'

In the meantime he appeared for France at the 1976 Montreal Olympics and two years later at the World Cup where, although he scored against hosts and future champions Argentina, he was unable to steer his country beyond the first round. His move to Saint Etienne came soon afterwards and in 1981 his 20 goals helped them to the French League title.

After scoring the decisive goal against Holland (an exquisite free-kick) to take France to the 1982 World Cup finals, Platini proceeded to reign in Spain. He was in magnificent form throughout the tournament, never more so than in the controversial semi-final with West Germany. It was he who scored the equalising penalty and displayed the whole range of his passing and organisational talents to drive the underdogs into a 3-1 lead, only for the French to be cheated out of their just desserts by a cynical and brutal challenge by German keeper Harald Schumacher on Patrick Battiston when the Frenchman was clean through on goal. Schumacher was allowed to stay on the pitch and the Germans eventually won on penalties . . . Schumacher making the crucial save. France may have lost the game but they won an army of neutral fans.

By the 1984 European Championships the French midfield of Platini, Jean Tigana and Alain Giresse was at its peak. Platini scored nine goals, including 'perfect' hat-tricks (a goal with either foot and one with his head) against both Belgium and Yugoslavia. His free-kick also opened the scoring in the final against Spain, France going on to win 2-0 to collect their first major international honour.

Michel Platini

Born: Joeuf, France, 1955

Country: France

International Caps: 72

International Goals: 41

Position: Midfield

Clubs: Joeuf, AS Nancy-Lorraine, Saint Etienne, Juventus

By now Platini was plying his trade in Italy, having joined Juventus immediately after the 1982 World Cup for £1.2 million. Wearing the famous black and white stripes of the 'Old Lady', he accumulated a host of titles and honours: two Italian Championships, one Coppa Italia, one European Cup, one European Cup Winners' Cup, and an unprecedented hat-trick of European Footballer of the Year awards. In those same three years (1983-85) he finished top goalscorer in Italy on each occasion. It was Platini's penalty that had won the 1985 European Cup Final against Liverpool, but the result was overshadowed by the Heysel Stadium disaster. 'That night had nothing to do with football,' he said later. 'They had to bring us the Cup in the dressing-room.'

After steering France to the semi-finals of the 1986 World Cup, Platini announced his retirement in order to concentrate on commercial and media work. He had scored 68 goals in 146 games for Juventus and in total had amassed 348 goals in 648 matches. In 1990 he was persuaded to return to football as French national team manager but quit after a disappointing 1992 European Championships. When France secured the privilege of hosting the 1998 World Cup, he again answered his country's call and became co-president of the French Organising Committee. On the pitch and off it, Michel Platini was the master organiser.

Michel Platini is manhandled by Bernd Forster during the 1982 World Cup match between France and West Germany. The Germans won 5-4 on penalties, the match having finished 3-3 after extra time.

FERENC PUSKAS

FERENC PUSKAS

Back in 1953 the widely held view – at least within these shores – was that England's footballers were the finest in the world. The embarrassing 1-0 defeat to the United States at the World Cup three years earlier was dismissed as a freak result. After all, a foreign team had yet to win at Wembley and nobody expected the Hungarian eleven that took to the hallowed turf on that grey November afternoon to be any different. Of particular amusement to the confident England fans in the pre-match kickabout was the 'fat little chap' in the Hungarian forward line. Just over 90 minutes later, England's proud record had been reduced to ashes as they were given a six-goal football lesson by the Magnificent Magyars. And the world had been introduced to the peculiar talent that was Ferenc Puskas.

By no stretch of the imagination did Puskas look like a finely honed athlete. He was short, overweight, couldn't head a ball and only used one foot. But that left foot was a magic wand with which he cast a bewitching spell over Billy Wright and Co. England's defenders were bred on man-for-man marking, as a result of which they were utterly

England captain Billy Wright (left) and Ferenc Puskas exchange before England's first ever home defeat at Wembley in 1953.

bewildered by Hungary's tactic of playing a deep-lying centre forward, Nandor Hidegkuti, allowing Puskas and Sandor Kocsis to push forward from the inside-forward positions. Whilst Hidegkuti hogged the headlines with a hat-trick, it was Puskas who pulled the strings and still found time to score twice himself, cruelly toying with the hapless England keeper Gil Merrick. The rules of football were rewritten that afternoon.

Puskas was born in Budapest and at the age of sixteen made his debut for his father's old team, Kispest. Two years later he made his international debut against Austria. With military teams springing up all over Eastern Europe, in 1948 the Hungarian authorities took all the Kispest players and turned them into Honved, the representatives of the nation's army. Honved romped to the League title in that first season, Puskas' 50 goals and the fact that he was an army officer playing for an army team earning him the nickname 'The Galloping Major'. Since Communist sports teams were considered amateurs, Puskas was able to captain his country to victory in the 1952 Olympics but their 1954 World Cup adventure ended in a shock defeat to West Germany in the final – the Hungarians' first loss for four years. The great team finally broke up during the Hungarian Revolution of 1956 when Puskas and others defected to the West. He had scored an astonishing 83 goals in 84 internationals.

Two years later he signed for his old Honved manager, Emil Oestreicher, who had taken over at Real Madrid and, although he was now the wrong side of 30, Puskas inspired Real to dominate Europe. Four times the leading scorer in the Spanish League, his finest hour came in the 1960 European Cup final when he scored four goals in Real's 7-3 annihilation of Eintracht Frankfurt. It was Real's fifth successive European Cup triumph and Puskas remains the only player to have scored four times in a European Cup Final. He also scored a hat-trick in the 1962 final but ended up on the losing side as Real went down 5-3 to Benfica. In total he scored 35 goals for Real in 39 European matches – a fantastic feat.

Bizarrely he represented a second country that year, playing for his adoptive Spain in the World Cup but it was a disappointing farewell to the international arena. He continued playing for Real until 1966 before retiring to concentrate on coaching and later guided unfancied Panathinaikos of Greece to the 1971 European Cup final. Then in 1993 he was briefly appointed caretaker manager of Hungary. It was a poignant moment. The star who had fled into exile nearly forty years earlier had finally been forgiven.

Ferenc Puskas

Born: Budapest, Hungary, 1927

Country: Hungary, Spain

International Caps: 88

International Goals: 83

Position: Inside forward

Clubs: Kispest, Honved, Real Madrid

ROBERTO RIVELINO

ROBERTO RIVELINO

A pre-match ritual for Isadore Irandir, goalkeeper with Rio Preto, was to say his prayers in the goalmouth. He adopted his customary pose at the start of a Brazilian League game with Corinthians and was still on his knees beseeching the Almighty when the ball whistled past his ear and into the back of the net. Just three seconds had been played. Irandir had forgotten that the Corinthians line-up included Roberto Rivelino, one of the most sensational strikers of a ball the world has ever seen. Rivelino's speciality was the banana free-kick, a shot which could almost turn right angles in flight, but he was equally adept at firing in long-range efforts in open play so a massive thumping drive from the half-way line into a vacant net posed few problems.

His other trick was the elastic dribble, which consisted of running the foot over the top of the ball, making it appear to swerve one side before sending it the other way. This proved a rich source of goals for him, often leaving defenders open-mouthed and wrong-footed in his wake. With such a repertoire of skills and his familiar bandit-like moustache, it was no wonder that Rivelino was such an instantly recognisable figure.

The Sao Paulo-born Rivelino spent almost his entire career with the local team Corinthians. He made his international debut against Uruguay at the age of 22 and his versatility (he could play in a variety of positions), coupled to his dribbling and power shooting marked him down as one to watch. However, Joao Saldanha, manager of the national team, seemed unsure about how best to use his explosive new talent with the result that Rivelino often had to be content with playing just 45 minutes. It was Rivelino's good fortune that Saldanha, whose tactics had come under increasing criticism, was replaced shortly before the 1970 World Cup by Mario Zagalo, a man who, whilst catering for the traditional Brazilian flair, also valued the importance of set pieces. With Pele being singled out for rough treatment, Brazil needed players who could withstand tough tackling. As well as providing that extra dimension from free-kicks, Rivelino could easily take care of himself.

Thus Rivelino was in favour when Brazil began their campaign in Mexico, forming part of a devastating forward line with Pele, Gerson, Jairzinho and Tostao. He marked the opening game with Czechoslovakia by scoring with a swerving 25-yarder and finished with three goals in the competition as Brazil swept to world domination.

Roberto Rivelino

Born: Sao Paulo, Brazil, 1946

Country: Brazil

International Caps: 96

International Goals: 44

Position: Midfield

Clubs: Corinthians, Fluminese, El Halal

By the time of the 1974 World Cup Brazil had lost many of their stars. The team struggled with Rivelino alone playing to his full potential. In a tournament that was devoid of the anticipated Brazilian flair, Rivelino conjured up a rare moment to remember when he lined up a free-kick against East Germany. Team-mate Jairzinho positioned himself in the German defensive wall and neatly ducked out of the way as Rivelino powered a typical banana bender around him and into the net. It was a beautifully worked routine.

Rivelino appeared for a third World Cup in 1978. He showed touches of brilliance – notably in the third place play-off against Italy – but generally looked overweight and unfit. It came as no surprise therefore when he announced his retirement shortly afterwards but not before becoming Brazil's then most capped player.

Rivelino spent ten years with Corinthians but was dismayed at not being able to win the Sao Paulo Championship. The fans appreciated his loyalty and nicknamed him 'Reizinho do Parque' ('Little King of the Park'). When it was finally time to move on, he joined Fluminese for three years before going to El Helal in Saudi Arabia to make some extra money at the end of his career. He went on to become a respected TV commentator in Brazil.

Rivelino's moustache gives an interview during the 1978 World Cup finals in Argentina.

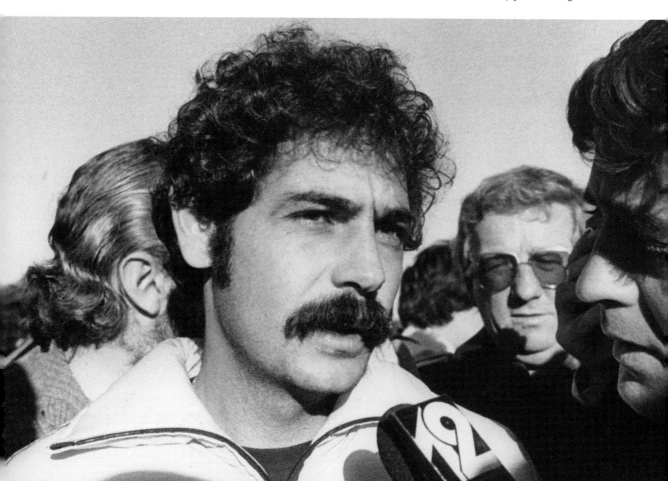

GIANNI RIVERA

Gianni Rivera

Born: Valle San
Bartolomeo, Italy, 1943

Country: Italy

International Caps: 60

International Goals: 14

Position: Midfield

Clubs: Alessandria,
AC Milan

GIANNI RIVERA

Few players have divided Italian public opinion more sharply than Gianni Rivera, the slim, skilful inside-forward known as 'The Golden Boy'. Many considered him to be the country's outstanding player of his era, a 'must' for the national side; others thought he was over-rated, over-indulged and distinctly lacking in courage. The result was that this stylish midfielder never really received the recognition he deserved.

Rivera moved with such poise that he seemed to float through matches on a cushion of air. His range of passing was unrivalled in Italy at the time and he possessed the ability to unlock the most fortress-like defence with one penetrating ball. And whilst he may have shirked the odd tackle, who could blame him, given the predominance of hatchet men in Italy in the 1960s?

Gianni Rivera was born in the Valle San Bartolomeo, a province of Alessandria, and it was with Alessandria that he made his Serie A debut against Inter Milan in June 1959. During that summer he was spotted by AC Milan's general manager Gipo Viani playing in an exhibition training game. It is said that Viani thought he was seeing double as the Uruguayan Juan Schiaffino – who had been rated one of the top five players in the world – was also playing and the two midfielders looked very similar in both physique and talent. Suitably impressed, Milan arranged for Rivera to join them at the end of the following season.

Rivera had played only 26 games for Alessandria (scoring six goals) so it was quite a step up but he took it all in his elegant stride. In only his second season in Milan, the eighteen-year-old helped the club to the League title and a year later he played a major part in the 2-1 European Cup Final victory over Benfica at Wembley, providing the pass for Jose Altafini to equalise Eusebio's goal. The next few years saw a downturn in fortunes for both Milan and Rivera, winning only the Coppa Italia in 1967. But the next year, with Rivera as captain, the club captured both the League title and the European Cup Winners' Cup. Further success followed in 1969 with a second European Cup (beating Ajax 4-1 in the final) and Rivera being voted European Footballer of the Year – the first native-born Italian to win the prestigious award.

Having helped an under-strength Italy to fourth place at the 1960 Rome Olympics, Rivera had made his debut with the full national side in 1962. He went on to play in four World Cup tournaments. He escaped blame for the poor showing in 1962 but was made a scapegoat for Italy's disastrous defeat at the hands of North Korea in 1966. Coach Ferruccio Valcareggi chose to leave Rivera out of the opening games in

1970 but he made his mark when coming on as substitute in the semi-final against West Germany, first committing the error that allowed Gerd Müller to tie the score at 3-3 and then scoring Italy's dramatic winner. Nevertheless he only appeared for the last six minutes of the final against Brazil. When the beaten finalists returned home they were greeted in true Italian fashion with a bombardment of rotten tomatoes, the exception being Rivera who was cheered by supporters puzzled as to why he had not been allowed to play a greater part in the tournament.

Rivera remained with Milan until 1979, scoring a total of 124 goals in 501 matches. During the seventies he picked up another European Cup Winners' Cup medal, a third League title and three more Italian Cups. He finished Serie A top scorer in 1973 (with seventeen goals) but in the same year accused the establishment and referees of colluding against Milan and favouring Juventus – remarks that led to a heavy fine and suspension. Given his aptitude for stirring up controversy, it came as no surprise when he went into Italian politics.

Gianni Rivera (left) with Karl-Heinz Schnellinger after Rivera had scored twice in extra time to help Italy beat West Germany 4-3 during the 1970 World Cup in Mexico.

Paolo Rossi scored a hat-trick in this World Cup encounter with Brazil in 1982, Italy winning 3-2.

PAOLO ROSSI

Paolo Rossi's career lay in shreds in 1980. Convicted of being involved in a match-fixing scandal that rocked Italian football, Rossi was banned from playing professional football for three years. The suspension plus ongoing knee problems threatened to terminate his playing days at 23 but he battled back from both to become a World Cup hero.

The teenage Rossi had been spotted by Turin giants Juventus but after two knee operations they loaned him out to Serie B outfit Como in the hope of toughening him up. It was when he was loaned to another Serie B team, Vicenza, in 1976 that he really exploded onto the scene. Converted from a winger to centre forward, he scored 21 goals to power the club to promotion in his first season, prompting Vicenza to splash out £1.5 million to make the move permanent. His 24 goals the following year caught the eye of national coach Enzo Bearzot who awarded him his first cap. He grabbed the chance with both hands, providing three goals and two assists at the 1978 World Cup in Argentina. A new star had arrived.

With the Rossi bandwagon on the roll, Vicenza sold him to Perugia for a world record £3 million but just when everything appeared to be going smoothly a 2-2 draw with lowly Avelino (in which Rossi scored both Perugia goals) began to arouse suspicion. Rossi and several team-mates were accused of fixing the result. Rossi strenuously denied the charge but was found guilty and suspended for three years, the sentence commuted to two on appeal. Suddenly he was cut off in his prime.

In 1981, while Rossi was still suspended, Juventus bought him back for a cut price £500,000. The ban ended on 29 April 1982, little over a month before the start of the World Cup, but Rossi was immediately recalled to the side. Bearzot later explained the decision: 'I knew that if Rossi wasn't in Spain, I wouldn't have had an opportunist inside the penalty box. In that area he was really good, really fast, always ready to fool defenders with his feints.'

GREAT FOOTBALL HEROES

PAOLO ROSSI

The fans and the media were sceptical, particularly after the first round matches where Italy scraped through after mustering just two goals in their three games. A narrow 2-1 victory over Argentina hinted at better things to come but Rossi had still to find the net. With the vultures circling, Bearzot decided to give him one last chance against Brazil who needed only a draw to reach the semi-final. Once again the world stage brought out the best in Rossi as he repaid his manager's faith with a spectacular hat-trick – a header and two instinctive strikes – as Italy went through 3-2. Rossi was on fire now. He scored both goals in the semi-final victory over Poland and the first against West Germany in the final. Italy were world champions and Rossi's six goals made him the tournament's leading scorer. His critics had to eat humble pie, swallowing an extra slice when he was voted European Footballer of the Year.

After helping Juventus win the European Cup Winners' Cup (against FC Porto in 1984) and the European Cup (against Liverpool in 1985), the Tuscan striker joined AC Milan. He made the squad for the 1986 World Cup but didn't play and after a brief spell with Verona, that recurring knee injury forced him to retire at the age of 31. He finished with 82 goals from 215 Serie A games.

Something of a loner off the field, Rossi disappeared from the world of football (apart from a scouting job with the Spanish national team) to devote his energies to his passion for deep-sea diving. For a player whose career had at one point plunged the depths it is quite an appropriate hobby.

Paolo Rossi

Born: Prato, Italy, 1956

Country: Italy

International Caps: 48

International Goals: 20

Position: Striker

Clubs: Juventus, Como, Vicenza, Perugia, AC Milan, Verona

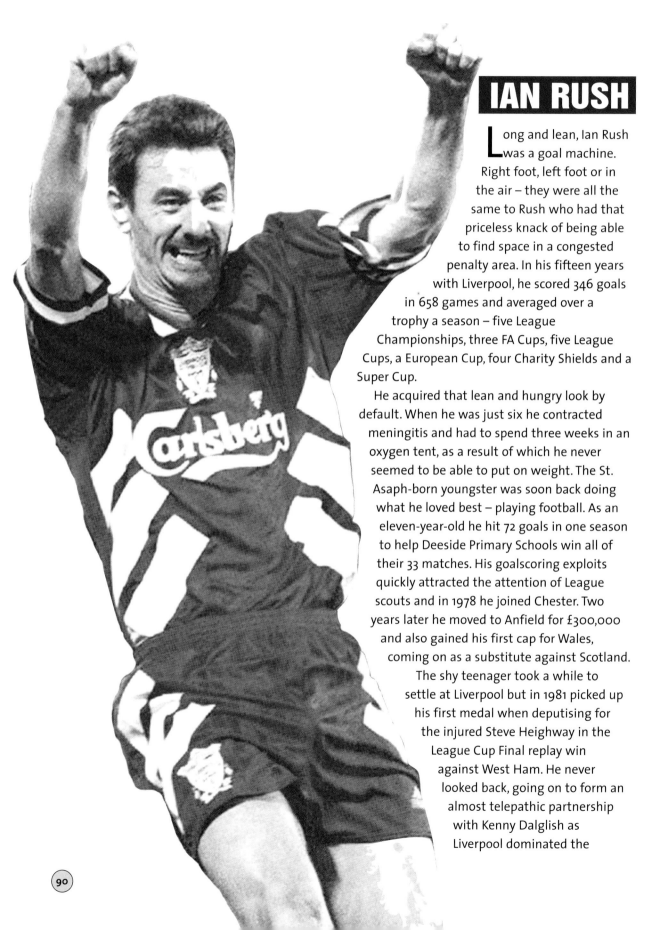

IAN RUSH

Long and lean, Ian Rush was a goal machine. Right foot, left foot or in the air – they were all the same to Rush who had that priceless knack of being able to find space in a congested penalty area. In his fifteen years with Liverpool, he scored 346 goals in 658 games and averaged over a trophy a season – five League Championships, three FA Cups, five League Cups, a European Cup, four Charity Shields and a Super Cup.

He acquired that lean and hungry look by default. When he was just six he contracted meningitis and had to spend three weeks in an oxygen tent, as a result of which he never seemed to be able to put on weight. The St. Asaph-born youngster was soon back doing what he loved best – playing football. As an eleven-year-old he hit 72 goals in one season to help Deeside Primary Schools win all of their 33 matches. His goalscoring exploits quickly attracted the attention of League scouts and in 1978 he joined Chester. Two years later he moved to Anfield for £300,000 and also gained his first cap for Wales, coming on as a substitute against Scotland. The shy teenager took a while to settle at Liverpool but in 1981 picked up his first medal when deputising for the injured Steve Heighway in the League Cup Final replay win against West Ham. He never looked back, going on to form an almost telepathic partnership with Kenny Dalglish as Liverpool dominated the domestic game for the remainder of the decade. Rush didn't only score goals himself – his selfless running off the ball enabled others to exploit the space behind him. His vintage year was 1984 when he and Liverpool won a third successive League Championship, a fourth successive League Cup and the European Cup. His total of 47 goals in all competitions that season (including 32 in the League) earned him Europe's Golden Boot and the award of Footballer of the Year. Above all, Rush specialised in hat-tricks, scoring no fewer than fifteen at senior level in the course of his career.

Like all great British players of the modern era, he was eager to discover whether he could perform to the same standard abroad. So a year after securing a fourth League title with Liverpool in 1986 and scoring two of the goals in the FA Cup Final victory over neighbours Everton (the team he had supported as a boy), he joined Juventus for £3.2 million. But he didn't settle and scored only seven League goals for the Italian giants. He later complained without a trace of irony: 'It was like being in a foreign country out there.'

In 1988 he returned to Anfield for £2.8 million and carried on where he had left off. He scored three more FA Cup Final goals (two in 1989 against Everton and one in 1992 against Sunderland) to create a record total of five in the Wembley showpiece. His total of 44 FA Cup goals is a twentieth century record. He shares with Geoff Hurst the all-time League Cup scoring record with 49 and was the first player to win that competition five times, completing his nap hand as Liverpool captain against Bolton Wanderers in 1995. In all he scored ten times in eighteen Wembley outings for Liverpool. When he was unusually on the losing side in the 1987 League Cup Final against Arsenal, it was the first time that Liverpool had ever been beaten in a game in which Rush had scored. He also created an all-time Mersey derby record of 25 goals against Everton and is Wales's record goalscorer.

Given a free transfer by Liverpool in 1996, he joined Leeds United but the goals dried up completely. It was the same at Newcastle and even Wrexham. Ian Rush was a spent force – but what a force he had been.

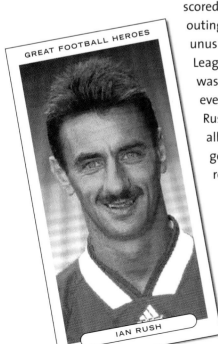

GREAT FOOTBALL HEROES

IAN RUSH

Opposite: Ian Rush celebrates after scoring his 41st FA Cup goal to equal Denis Law's post-war record in the competition as Liverpool defeated Wimbledon 2-0.

Ian Rush

Born: St. Asaph, Wales, 1961

Country: Wales

International Caps: 73

International Goals: 28

Position: Striker

Clubs: Chester, Liverpool, Juventus, Leeds United, Newcastle, Wrexham, Sydney Olympic

JUAN SCHIAFFINO

Juan Schiaffino is generally regarded as the finest player ever to come out of Uruguay. Although only slightly built, he defied those who thought he would be crushed by some of the most rugged, intimidating defenders in world soccer and went on to become a highly accomplished inside-forward. In that role he was able to demonstrate his tremendous repertoire of passing, allied to a fierce shot, extraordinary vision and lightning speed.

Born in Montevideo, he broke into the Peñarol youth team as a

Juan Schiaffino (front row third from right) lines up with the World Cup-winning Uruguayan team of 1950.

seventeen-year-old and a year later had progressed to the first eleven. Ten days before his twentieth birthday he made his international debut against Argentina in the South American Championship, a competition which the Uruguayans went on to win.

The 1950 World Cup was decided by a four-team pool rather than a final match. After 7-1 and 6-1 wins against Sweden and Spain respectively, Brazil (the tournament favourites and host nation) needed only a draw from their last game with Uruguay to win the World Cup. By contrast,

Uruguay had only drawn 2-2 with Spain and stumbled to a 3-2 victory over Sweden and were consequently ranked 10-1 outsiders. Brazil were so confident that the Rio de Janeiro state governor proclaimed them as champions and they had a victory song written in advance. Any football song is a mistake but this one doubly so. Yet at first everything went according to the script and when Friaça put Brazil ahead just before half-time, the trophy appeared theirs for the taking. But, throwing caution to the wind, Uruguay fought back and Schiaffino equalised midway through the second half before setting up a dramatic winner for Chico Ghiggia with just eleven minutes left. Uruguay had won the World Cup for the second time, Schiaffino finishing on five goals.

Schiaffino was once again Uruguay's key player in the 1954 tournament. With him at his best, anything was possible but without him they struggled. He gave notice of his intentions by scoring against Czechoslovakia and then in the 4-2 victory over England as Uruguay advanced smoothly to the semi-finals. However, in the semi-final against Hungary, the Uruguayans were hampered by an injury to Schiaffino and were beaten 4-2 in extra-time – their first defeat in a World Cup match. Depleted and demoralised, they promptly lost to Austria in the third place play-off.

Later that year Schiaffino moved to AC Milan for a world record fee of £72,000, helping the club to three League Championships and the 1958 European Cup Final in Brussels where they lost 3-2 after extra-time to the all-conquering Real Madrid. Revelling in the big match atmosphere, Schiaffino scored one of the Milan goals. Six months after his transfer he played the first of four internationals for his adopted country, having been called up to boost Italy's World Cup qualifying campaign, but it ended in disappointment as they failed to reach the finals in Sweden. But he remains one of the few players to have appeared in World Cup matches for more than one country.

At the age of 34 he moved to AS Roma and spent two seasons in the Italian capital before retiring in 1962. Although the brain was as quick and incisive as ever, the legs were no longer as willing. After almost fifteen years away from the game, Schiaffino suddenly returned to the spotlight to take charge of his old club Peñarol in 1976 and later had a brief spell as the Uruguayan national coach. Sadly, the players failed to measure up to the coach's high standards.

A throwback to the old days of the scheming inside-forward, in his prime Schiaffino often appeared to be an artist among honest labourers. Uruguay may have produced thousands of players down the years but there was only Juan Schiaffino.

GREAT FOOTBALL HEROES

JUAN SCHIAFFINO

Juan Schiaffino

Born: Montevideo, Uruguay, 1925 (d.2002)

Country: Uruguay, Italy

International Caps: 49

International Goals: 12

Position: Inside forward

Clubs: Peñarol, AC Milan, AS Roma

Uwe Seeler

Born: Hamburg, Germany, 1936

Country: Germany

International Caps: 72

International Goals: 43

Position: Centre forward

Clubs: Hamburg

UWE SEELER

Back in the 1960s the most familiar sound in German football was the chant of 'Uwe, Uwe' cascading down from the stands and terraces. The object of this adulation was a stocky little man with receding hair. His name was Uwe Seeler and in shape, size, attitude, and goal poaching ability, he was very much the prototype for Gerd Müller.

Until Müller came along, Seeler was West Germany's most prolific goalscorer. He possibly lacked a little of his successor's technique in the box but made up for it with sheer hard graft and a never-say-die approach that enabled him to turn apparently lost causes into strikes on goal. Seeler would chase anything, snapping at the heels of defenders like a Jack Russell, nagging them into mistakes. And once he was given a sight of goal there were few more precise finishers than the little man from Hamburg.

The son of a former Hamburg player, Seeler remained with the club throughout his professional career, repeatedly rejecting overtures from leading clubs in Italy and Spain. He made his League debut in 1953 and within a year had worn the national shirt for the first time, coming on

as a seventeen-year-old substitute against France. His first start for the reigning world champions was in December 1954 at Wembley. England won 3-1 that day. Seeler's revenge would come sixteen years later.

By the time of the 1958 World Cup in Sweden, Seeler was a regular in the side and scored twice as West Germany reached the semi-finals before losing to the hosts. The following year he scored his first international hat-trick in the 7-0 rout of Holland – there would be two more, against Denmark in 1961 and Turkey in 1963.

In 1960 he became West Germany's first Footballer of the Year and in 1961 he captained Hamburg to the semi-final of the European Cup where they lost to Barcelona. Despite winning the German Cup in 1963, major honours continued to elude him. The following year was the first of the unified Bundesliga. Seeler had scored an incredible 267 goals in 237 matches for Hamburg in the old regional Premier League North, seven times finishing as the League's top scorer, and now he set about emulating those achievements nationally. In that first Bundesliga season, Seeler was the leading scorer with 30 goals – one of four occasions on which he would head the Bundesliga charts. When his playing career ended in 1972, he had scored 137 goals in 239 Bundesliga matches. Further West German Footballer of the Year awards followed in 1964 and 1970 and in 1968 he captained Hamburg to the final of the European Cup Winners' Cup. Again it ended in defeat, however, AC Milan running out the 2-0 winners.

It was left to the international team, therefore, to produce the honours that Seeler's honest endeavour surely merited. He scored twice in the 1962 World Cup finals, only for the Germans to succumb to Yugoslavia in the quarter-finals, and then captained the side in the 1966 tournament. He produced two goals *en route* to the final – against Spain and Uruguay – but that Russian linesman at Wembley ensured another disappointment for Seeler. He scored in his fourth finals in 1970 (a record he shares with Pele), and notched two other goals in Mexico, most famously his hopeful back header that looped over Peter Bonetti for West Germany's equaliser in the quarter-final against England. His joy was short-lived, however, as the Germans lost to Italy in the semi-finals. He played just one more game – against Hungary — before hanging up his international boots.

It was Uwe Seeler's misfortune that his international career spanned the gap between West Germany's first World Cup success in 1954 and their victory on home soil in 1974. As Seeler would acknowledge, in football timing is everything.

Opposite: *Russia's Lev Yashin intercepts a Uwe Seeler strike during the 1966 World Cup.* Above: *A programme from the 1966 World Cup final.*

PETER SHILTON

PETER SHILTON

It may sound unlikely for anyone who played for years under Brian Clough but Peter Shilton's biggest critic was invariably himself. Shilton was a perfectionist who, from an early age, strove to develop his physique and agility so that he could become the best goalkeeper in the game. His reward was a career spanning over 30 years in which he won a record number of England caps and became the first player to reach the milestone of 1,000 Football League appearances.

He made his debut in 1966 for Leicester City and showed such promise that the club allowed England's number one, Gordon Banks, to leave so that the youngster's career could progress. After playing in his one and only FA Cup Final – a 1-0 defeat by Manchester City in 1969 – Shilton kept a club record 23 clean sheets in 1970-71 and was rewarded with his first England call-up against East Germany. However, the

ambitious Shilton was becoming worried by Leicester's lack of progress and in 1974 the club sold their unhappy star for £325,000 to Stoke City where he once again followed in Banks' footsteps. Ironically, Stoke fared no better and when they were relegated to the Second Division, Shilton was snapped up by Brian Clough at Nottingham Forest.

With his command of the area, shot-stopping ability and sound positional sense, Shilton played a major role in Forest's success over the next five years, picking up two European Cups, a League title and a League Cup win. Then, in 1982, he was on his way again, to Southampton.

England manager Ron Greenwood had frequently alternated Shilton with Ray Clemence (thereby costing Shilton many more caps) but by the 1982 World Cup in Spain, he had finally made up his mind that Shilton was first choice. Shilton enjoyed an excellent tournament, conceding just one goal in five matches. He played again in the 1986 World Cup, only to be robbed by Maradona's 'Hand of God' goal.

An England fixture (he even captained the side on occasions), Shilton maintained his impeccable standards while pursuing his goal of breaking appearance records at domestic and international level. In 1987 he made his last big money move – to Derby County – and in April 1988 overtook Terry Paine's all-time record of 824 Football League appearances. And when he was selected to play against Denmark in June 1989, Shilton broke Bobby Moore's record of 108 England caps. Shilton was now in a league of his own.

He had no intention of hanging up his boots yet and his safe hands and general presence inspired England to reach the semi-finals of the 1990 World Cup, only for his dreams of appearing in the final to be shattered by Chris Waddle blasting a penalty into the stratosphere. Immediately after the tournament Shilton decided to quit the international scene while he was at the top. In those 125 matches, he conceded just 80 goals and kept a record 65 clean sheets.

In 1992 he became player/manager of Plymouth Argyle but whilst his playing skills were not in question, his management skills were and he was sacked three years later. Stuck on the 995 mark for League appearances, he made a concerted effort to reach the elusive figure, joining Wimbledon, Bolton Wanderers, Coventry City and then West Ham as cover. Finally on 22 December 1996, at the age of 47, he made his 1,000[th] League appearance when turning out for Leyton Orient against Brighton. True to form he kept a clean sheet. He went on to raise his total to 1,005 before Orient manager Pat Holland released him on the grounds that he 'couldn't kick the ball far enough'. Peter Shilton had finally found a tougher critic than himself.

Opposite: *Peter Shilton in action for England in 1973 on his way to earning a record number of international caps.*

Peter Shilton

Born: Leicester, England, 1949

Country: England

International Caps: 125

International Goals: 0

Position: Goalkeeper

Clubs: Leicester City, Stoke City, Nottingham Forest, Southampton, Derby County, Plymouth Argyle, Wimbledon, Bolton Wanderers, Coventry City, West Ham, Leyton Orient

FRANK SWIFT

Frank Swift was a big man in every sense. Standing 6ft 2in tall and weighing fourteen stone, the legendary Manchester City and England goalkeeper had a finger span of nearly twelve inches, enabling him to grasp a ball in one hand with relative ease. He was also a cheerful, larger-than-life character who was greatly mourned when he tragically lost his life in the 1958 Munich air crash.

Born in Blackpool, Swift started out playing for the local gasworks team where he worked as a coke-keeper. Moving up the ladder, he played as an amateur for Fleetwood Town before turning professional and signing for Manchester City in October 1932 on wages of ten shillings a week. However, after three impressive performances for the reserves, he was given a pay rise and eventually promoted to the first team, making his debut against Derby County on Christmas Day 1933 — just one day short of his twentieth birthday. He played 22 games in the second half of that season, culminating in a Wembley appearance when City met Portsmouth in the 1934 FA Cup Final. As the referee blew the final whistle to signal City's 2-1 triumph, Swift was so overcome with emotion that he fainted on his goal-line but recovered in time to collect his medal from King George V.

Between 1934 and the outbreak of war, 'Big Swifty' only missed one game for City. He was a safe but spectacular goalkeeper who, once he had overcome the nerves from the start of his career, enjoyed nothing more than playing up to the fans. He explained: 'I threw in a bit of showmanship to please the crowd. Football's only a game, after all.' Swift was also one of the first keepers to opt for throwing the ball to team-mates rather than booting it up the field and many a City attack stemmed from his pioneering method of distribution. In 1937 he helped City win the League Championship but hopes of further honours were dashed by the war. At the start of hostilities Swift enrolled as a special constable in charge of traffic control but gave it up on the first day. Despite the interruption to his career, he still managed to make over 150 unofficial appearances for City and appear in ten wartime internationals for England.

Swift's pre-war form had been exceptional yet he was repeatedly overlooked for England honours until 1947 when he finally made his debut against Scotland. In May of the following year he became the first goalkeeper ever to captain England when he led the team on to the field against mighty Italy in Turin. The decision had been roundly criticised as it was feared that a goalkeeper would be too remote from the play to encourage his team. But as Swift later pointed out: 'Captaincy is not a matter of hand-clapping and shouting. It is a matter of confidence and comradeship in one another.' He remembered his nerves jangling in the dressing-room beforehand until Stanley Matthews walked over to him, shook his hand and said quietly: 'I'll give you everything I've got tonight, Frank.' One by one the other players all did the same. England went out and routed the Italians 4-0. It was Swift's finest hour.

He played his last international in 1949 against Norway, having kept nine clean sheets in his 19 matches. In the same year he stopped playing domestic football after 338 League appearances for City – his only club – although his registration was not cancelled for another six years.

He turned to coaching and became a respected soccer journalist for the *News of the World*. One of his assignments was to cover Manchester United's progress in the European Cup campaign of 1958. Sadly it was to be his last.

GREAT FOOTBALL HEROES

FRANK SWIFT

Opposite: *England goalkeeper Frank Swift was one of the first keepers to adopt the practice of throwing the ball to team-mates rather than kicking it.*

Frank Swift

Born: Blackpool, England, 1913 (d. 1958)

Country: England

International Caps: 19

International Goals: 0

Position: Goalkeeper

Clubs: Manchester City

GREAT FOOTBALL HEROES

MARCO VAN BASTEN

MARCO VAN BASTEN

Marco Van Basten was no disciple of the Dutch ideal of Total Football. He was not one for drifting into midfield or out on to the wing *à la* Cruyff but instead was a goalscorer pure and simple. As Cruyff himself once remarked: 'He doesn't influence the play very much, but he decides matches.'

And when it came to scoring goals, particularly ones that decided important matches, nobody did it better than Van Basten. This tall, athletic striker lit up the 1988 European Championships with a hat-trick against England, a late winner against West Germany in the semi-finals and a memorable angled volley in the final against the USSR to secure a 2-0 victory for Holland. Yet he had started the tournament as only his team's third choice striker.

The Marco Goalo story began in Utrecht but it was the Amsterdam giants Ajax who signed the teenager after spotting him at the club's annual youth talent gala. His first appearance for Ajax was as a substitute for the great Cruyff and by 1986 he was Europe's leading marksman, his 37 goals that season earning him the coveted Golden Boot. With Van Basten spearheading their attack, Ajax carried off two Dutch Championships, two Dutch Cups and, in 1987, the European Cup Winners' Cup at the expense of Lokomotiv Leipzig. Naturally Van Basten scored the only goal of the game. The following season he moved to AC Milan for £1.5 million, having scored an astonishing 128 League goals for Ajax in just 143 appearances.

Forming a formidable partnership with fellow Dutch striker Ruud Gullit, Van Basten helped Milan to their first Serie A title in nine years, although his appearances were severely restricted by an ankle injury. More significantly, his goals enabled Arrigo Sacchi's team to lift successive European Cups in 1989 and 1990, Van Basten scoring twice against Steaua Bucharest in the first of those finals. In the wake of the European Championships the accolades flowed thick and fast – European Footballer of the Year in 1988, 1989 and 1992; World Footballer of the Year in 1988 and 1992; and FIFA World Player of the Year in 1992.

He continued to re-write the record books, his spree against Malta in 1990 making him the first Dutch player to score five goals in an official international. A rare lapse occurred in the 1992 European Championships when he missed a decisive penalty in the semi-final shoot-out against Denmark. Holland were eliminated and Van Basten announced his retirement from international football shortly afterwards.

Domestically, he helped Milan to two more League titles, galvanised

Marco Van Basten

Born: Utrecht, Netherlands, 1964

Country: Holland

International Caps: 58

International Goals: 24

Position: Striker

Clubs: Ajax, AC Milan

by a purple patch of thirteen goals in fifteen games against the meanest defences in club football. However, amid all this success a dark cloud loomed on the horizon. The ankle injury – a legacy of being hacked mercilessly by tough-tackling defenders – flared up again, necessitating two operations. What would turn out to be his last competitive game was Milan's contentious 1-0 defeat by Olympique Marseille in the 1993 European Cup Final. Marseille were subsequently stripped of the victory and their French League title after the club's owner, Bernard Tapie, was found guilty of paying three Valenciennes players to take it easy in a League match a week before the European final.

Marco Van Basten clutches the trophy after Holland beat the USSR 2-0 in the final of the 1988 European Championship.

Van Basten eventually gave up on his struggle to regain fitness in August 1995 and was forced to retire from the game at the age of 30. He had scored 90 goals in 147 matches for Milan and had set a European Cup record haul of eighteen goals in 23 games for the club. He was also the leading marksman twice in Serie A.

Other players may have scored more spectacular goals but when it came to the big occasion, no one could match Marco Van Basten.

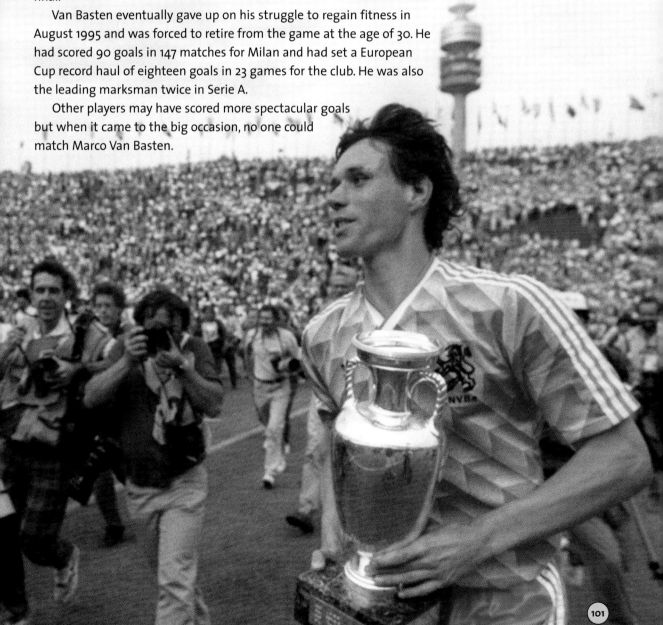

BILLY WRIGHT

BILLY WRIGHT

William Ambrose Wright was one of football's gentlemen. A one-club man, he was the first player to win 100 caps for his country and achieved the remarkable feat of winning 70 caps in a row between October 1951 and May 1959. Solid, composed and unflappable, he set yet another record by captaining England on no fewer than 90 occasions. And throughout his career he was never even booked.

Yet the man who would become the backbone of England's defence in the 1950s started out as a centre forward. Born in Ironbridge, Shropshire, he starred in attack for his school team and scored ten goals in one game. He was an Arsenal supporter as a boy but when he read in his local newspaper that Wolverhampton Wanderers were advertising for youngsters to go to Molineux for trials, he jumped at the opportunity. After being accepted on an eight-month trial, the fourteen-year-old turned out for Wolves in a B team game in the Walsall Minor League. At first the club's authoritarian manager, Major Frank Buckley, was unsure of Wright's talents and told him that he didn't think he was big enough to make the grade as a professional footballer. Fortunately for Wolves and England, Buckley had a change of heart.

The start of Wright's career was put on hold by the war, in which he served as an army physical training instructor, but when peace was restored he quickly established himself in the Wolves line-up and in 1947 was appointed club captain upon the retirement of Stan Cullis. Wright proved a quiet but inspirational leader, captaining Wolves to victory over Leicester City in the 1949 FA Cup Final and then to their first ever League Championship in 1954. In the meantime he was voted Footballer of the Year in 1952. Employing the physical long-ball game adopted by Stan Cullis, who had become the club's manager, Wolves emerged as *the* British team of the fifties. Two more

Billy Wright

Born: Ironbridge, England, 1924 (d. 1994)

Country: England

International Caps: 105

International Goals: 3

Position: Defence

Clubs: Wolverhampton Wanderers

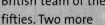

League titles were collected in 1958 and 1959 while Wolves also pioneered the staging of games against crack European opposition.

Wright played his first full international against Scotland at Wembley in 1947 and from then on became a fixture in the side thanks to his clean tackling and neat passing. However, whilst England excelled at thrashing mediocre opposition in meaningless friendlies, they failed to deliver when it really mattered and Wright's tenure coincided with some embarrassing setbacks to national pride, notably the defeat to the United States at the 1950 World Cup and the dual thrashings by Hungary in 1953 and 1954. The 1954 and 1958 World Cup adventures also ended in failure but the following year Wright reached that 100-cap milestone against Scotland. He played the last of his 541 games for Wolves against Leicester City at the end of 1958-59 and announced his retirement shortly before the start of the next season after being dropped in a friendly. His last international was also in 1959, ironically against the United States, having missed just three games since winning his first cap twelve years earlier.

With his marriage to Joy Beverley of the Beverley Sisters (they were the Posh and Becks of their day), Wright maintained his high profile, all the more so when he took over as manager of his boyhood heroes, Arsenal, in 1962. He met with only modest success, however, and left four years later to begin a media career with the Midlands company ATV. In May 1990, a year after his retirement as a television executive, he delighted Wolves fans by returning to the club as a director. It was a joyous homecoming. And when he died in September 1994, following an unsuccessful fight against cancer, his funeral brought the centre of Wolverhampton to a standstill. The town had not forgotten its favourite footballing son.

Wolves captain Billy Wright in action at Molineux in 1959.

LEV YASHIN

Known in Europe as the 'Black Panther' because of his distinctive all-black strip, Lev Yashin has been hailed as the finest goalkeeper in the history of football. Whilst others may also lay claim to that particular title, there can be no doubt that the man who saved no fewer than 150 penalties in his career is the most famous sportsman that the Soviet Union has ever produced.

Born into a family of Moscow factory workers, Yashin himself worked in a tools factory while playing amateur football in his spare time. Since he was the tallest boy in the neighbourhood, he wanted to play at centre forward but his team coach had other ideas and put him in goal. In 1946 he joined the Moscow Dynamo club . . . as an ice hockey goaltender. However, the coaches there soon realised that his natural aptitude was for soccer and after making his first-team debut in 1951, he took over as regular goalkeeper two years later when Alexei 'Tiger' Khomich suffered a long-term injury.

He gained his first international cap in 1954, helped his country to Olympic gold in 1956 and then to victory in the inaugural European Championships of 1960, beating Yugoslavia in the Paris final. By then Yashin was established as an outstanding goalkeeper, his agility complemented by sound positional sense. He was also one of the first keepers to be comfortable with playing outside the penalty area, his kicking being of the highest order. Nor did he hesitate when it came to organising the defenders in front of him – even his wife used to accuse him of shouting too much on the pitch. Although supremely confident he was incredibly superstitious and always took two caps to a match – one to wear and the other to put in the back of the net for luck.

Following an indifferent World Cup in 1962 where he made a few uncharacteristic blunders, as a result of which the USSR lost in the quarter-finals to host nation Chile, Yashin returned to form and was named European Footballer of the Year in 1963 – the only goalkeeper ever to have received that honour. He was also chosen to represent FIFA in a World XI at Wembley in a match to mark the centenary of the Football Association. He excelled in the 1966 World Cup although ironically it was his error that allowed West Germany's Franz Beckenbauer to score the decisive goal in the semi-finals. The next year he won the last of his 78 caps (then a Soviet record), having conceded under a goal a game during his thirteen years as national custodian.

Such was the esteem in which Yashin was held in his homeland that in 1968 he became the first footballer to be awarded the Soviet Union's highest honour, the Order of Lenin, and when he retired in 1970 the event was marked with a testimonial match the following year at the Lenin stadium in Moscow in front of 100,000 fans. An indication of the respect he enjoyed throughout the football world was the fact that players of the calibre of Pele, Eusebio, Bobby Charlton and Beckenbauer travelled to Moscow for the occasion. He had made 326 appearances for Moscow Dynamo, guiding them to five League titles and three domestic Cup successes. His reward was to be offered the manager's job the day after his testimonial.

Sadly, this supreme athlete, who had always covered the ground with such speed and purpose, was stricken by ill health in 1986 and had to have a leg amputated. He died four years later.

A true one-club man, his impact on Soviet sport cannot be over-estimated. At a time when supposedly female Russian shot putters had a nasty habit of disappearing off the face of the earth as soon as sex tests were introduced, Yashin was one of the few Soviet sporting heroes who was instantly recognisable and welcomed in the western world.

GREAT FOOTBALL HEROES

LEV YASHIN

Opposite: Lev Yashin saves a West German free kick during the 1966 World Cup semi final at Goodison Park.

Lev Yashin

Born: Moscow, USSR, 1929 (d. 1990)

Country: Soviet Union

International Caps: 78

International Goals: 0

Position: Goalkeeper

Clubs: Moscow Dynamo

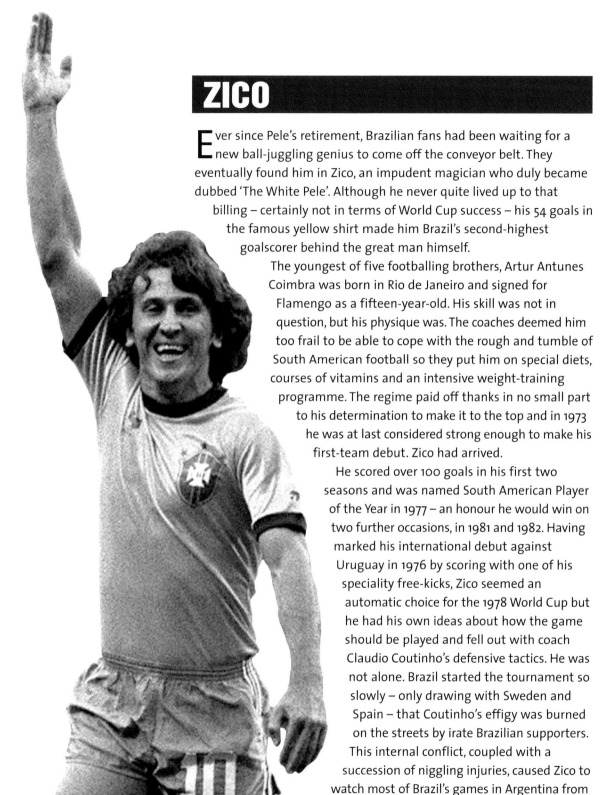

ZICO

Ever since Pele's retirement, Brazilian fans had been waiting for a new ball-juggling genius to come off the conveyor belt. They eventually found him in Zico, an impudent magician who duly became dubbed 'The White Pele'. Although he never quite lived up to that billing – certainly not in terms of World Cup success – his 54 goals in the famous yellow shirt made him Brazil's second-highest goalscorer behind the great man himself.

The youngest of five footballing brothers, Artur Antunes Coimbra was born in Rio de Janeiro and signed for Flamengo as a fifteen-year-old. His skill was not in question, but his physique was. The coaches deemed him too frail to be able to cope with the rough and tumble of South American football so they put him on special diets, courses of vitamins and an intensive weight-training programme. The regime paid off thanks in no small part to his determination to make it to the top and in 1973 he was at last considered strong enough to make his first-team debut. Zico had arrived.

He scored over 100 goals in his first two seasons and was named South American Player of the Year in 1977 – an honour he would win on two further occasions, in 1981 and 1982. Having marked his international debut against Uruguay in 1976 by scoring with one of his speciality free-kicks, Zico seemed an automatic choice for the 1978 World Cup but he had his own ideas about how the game should be played and fell out with coach Claudio Coutinho's defensive tactics. He was not alone. Brazil started the tournament so slowly – only drawing with Sweden and Spain – that Coutinho's effigy was burned on the streets by irate Brazilian supporters. This internal conflict, coupled with a succession of niggling injuries, caused Zico to watch most of Brazil's games in Argentina from the bench. And when he did get on, against Sweden, his last-gasp header from a corner was controversially disallowed by Welsh referee Clive Thomas who maintained that he had blown the whistle for full-time a split second before the ball flew into the net.

Better times lay ahead in 1981 when Zico's eleven goals helped Flamengo win the South American Club Cup (the Copa Libertadores) and they also went on to capture the World Club Cup, crushing Liverpool 3-0 in Tokyo. With Zico in sparkling form and Brazil returning to a more attacking style under Tele Santana, they looked a sound bet for the 1982 World Cup in Spain. Zico's hat-trick against Bolivia clinched a place in the finals where he scored four more goals, including the equaliser against Scotland who were eventually beaten 4-1. His body swerves, sudden changes of pace and dynamic shooting were a joy to watch but unfortunately for Brazil they came up against Paolo Rossi on one of his glory days and it was Italy who progressed to the semi-finals.

After 650 goals and four Championship medals with Flamengo, Zico joined Italian club Udinese for £2.5 million. That year (1983) saw him voted World Footballer of the Year but by the summer of 1985 he was back with Flamengo. Injury restricted him to just three substitute appearances at the 1986 World Cup finals. In the quarter-final against France he was brought on after the fans chanted his name but he promptly missed a crucial penalty and Brazil were on the way out. It was Zico's last match for his country – a sad end for such a popular player.

He retired in 1990 – having played 1,047 senior games – and was appointed Brazil's Sports Minister but a year later he made a surprise comeback, moving to Kashima Antlers of Japan where he helped to establish the new J-League. He returned to Brazil in 1997 and was appointed assistant coach to the national team, serving in that capacity at the following year's World Cup.

GREAT FOOTBALL HEROES

ZICO

Opposite: *Zico celebrates after scoring the only goal during a friendly football match between England and Brazil at Wembley in 1981.*

Zico

Born: Rio de Janeiro, Brazil, 1953

Country: Brazil

International Caps: 88

International Goals: 54

Position: Midfield

Clubs: Flamengo, Udinese Kashima Antlers

Dino Zoff

Born: Mariano del Friuli, Italy, 1942

Country: Italy

International Caps: 112

International Goals: 0

Position: Goalkeeper

Clubs: Udinese, Mantova, Napoli, Juventus

Opposite: Dino Zoff captained Italy to victory in the 1982 World Cup, the Italians beating Germany 3-1 in the final in Madrid.

DINO ZOFF

Italy's finest-ever goalkeeper holds two proud records. At 40, he was the oldest player to collect a World Cup winner's medal when he captained his country to victory in 1982. And between September 1972 and June 1974 he achieved the longest shut-out in international football, going 1,142 minutes without conceding a goal, a total of twelve matches. In the unlucky thirteenth – at the 1974 World Cup – he was beaten by a goal from Haiti of all teams!

Zoff would not have celebrated the record, he would have bemoaned the fact that he let in a goal. For he was a perfectionist, a workaholic who strove to be the best and was never satisfied with anything less.

A country boy from the agricultural north-east of Italy, Zoff was rejected by both Inter Milan and Juventus as a fourteen-year-old on the familiar grounds that he was too small. So his grandmother fed him on a steady diet of eggs and he shot up. Five years on and Zoff's displays for his village team, Marianese, prompted nearby Udinese to give him a chance. He packed in his job as a car mechanic to sign professional forms, making his debut in 1961 at Fiorentina . . . where he let in five goals and was immediately dropped. He played only four games for Udinese in two years before Mantova put him out of his misery. Four years and 67 League games with Mantova put Zoff in the shop window and in 1967 he hit the big time with a move south to Napoli.

Naples was to prove a lucky city for him, not least because it was the setting for his international debut in 1968 as Italy met Bulgaria in the quarter-finals of the European Championships. Italy won 2-0 and Zoff kept his place as the team went on to beat Yugoslavia in the final. He was surprisingly ousted for the 1970 World Cup and two years later moved in a £500,000 deal to Juventus with whom he would win six League titles, two Italian Cups and, in 1977, the UEFA Cup.

Meanwhile that superb run of clean sheets had ensured that Zoff would start the 1974 World Cup as Italy's number one but despite his outstanding form, the team exited at the group stage. Four years later he was determined to put that disappointment behind him, only to be the fall guy against Holland as first Ernie Brandts and then

GREAT FOOTBALL HEROES

DINO ZOFF

Arie Haan beat him with phenomenal strikes from long range. Many thought that would be Zoff's farewell on the international scene but he maintained his form for Juventus where he was a virtual ever-present during his eleven-year stay. As captain, Zoff led Italy into the 1982 World Cup in Spain and after surviving a fearful battering from Brazil, collected the coveted trophy on the back of victory over West Germany in the final. He thus became the second Juventus keeper to captain Italy to World Cup success, following in the footsteps of Gianpiero Combi back in 1934.

Having made 570 appearances in Serie A and achieved his lifetime's ambition, Zoff retired from playing in 1983 to become goalkeeping coach at Juventus. He found the role unfulfilling, describing it as 'a dead-end job', but jumped at the chance to coach the Italian team for the 1988 Seoul Olympics. He impressed sufficiently to be asked back to Juventus, this time as manager but despite winning an Italian Cup and the UEFA Cup within the space of a few weeks, he was soon on his way to Lazio. First as coach and latterly as president, he oversaw the revival of the Rome club but could not resist the lure of taking over the national team in 1998. Although he took Italy to the final of Euro 2000, he was stung by criticism following the cruel defeat to France and resigned. Dino Zoff always was a proud man.

BRAZIL

In world football Brazil are the supreme entertainers. For over half a century they have been synonymous with adventurous attacking play, outrageous ball skills and occasionally haphazard defending to win the hearts of armchair enthusiasts from Stockholm to Sydney. They play football the way it is meant to be played – on the ground rather than in the air, with brains not brawn, and with forward flair not stifling defensive tactics. And when occasionally they slip from their pedestal so that they merely rank alongside the best of the rest, we forgive them, knowing that another great Brazilian side is sure to come along soon.

It is no exaggeration to say that football is a religion in Brazil. In an impoverished country, the success of the national team has always been a source of immense pride. But whilst winning is important to the Brazilian public, winning with style is essential. It is the Brazilian way, the only way.

Although they had finished third at the 1938 World Cup thanks to the goals of their first real star, Léonidas, it was not until the 1950s that Brazil truly emerged as a world force. In 1950 they finished runners-up in the World Cup after being surprisingly beaten on home soil by Uruguay in front of 200,000 disbelieving fans, but eight years later, armed with a pioneering 4-2-4 formation and an unknown seventeen-year-old named Pele, they carried all before them, hammering hosts Sweden 5-2 in the final. It was exhibition stuff.

Brazil 1970. Captained by Carlos Alberto (standing, far left) the all-star World Cup winners were managed by Mario Zagalo who had been part of the first victorious World Cup team in 1958.

Overcoming the absence of Pele, injured in a group match with Czechoslovakia, Brazil retained their title in Chile in 1962. This time it was Garrincha and Vava who were the architects of victory. Consequently there was huge anticipation when the tournament came to England in

1966, only for Brazil – and Pele in particular – to fall foul of over-physical European opponents. To the disappointment of all neutrals, Brazil exited after the first round of matches.

The Brazilians of 1970 boasted the finest attacking line-up ever seen in world soccer. From Carlos Alberto, the rangy full-back who seemed to get from one end of the pitch to the other in a few loping strides, to the likes of Pele, Jairzinho, Tostao and Rivelino, every player in that Brazilian team was an artist. England's endeavour gave Brazil a run for their money in a group match – and but for a poor miss by the late Jeff Astle would have earned a draw – but thereafter the Brazilians were irresistible. Following the 4-1 annihilation of Italy in the final, jubilant fans mobbed the Brazilian team with such enthusiasm that Rivelino collapsed under the weight of the celebrations and had to be carried to the dressing-room on a stretcher!

The 1970 team proved a tough act to follow. Successive Brazilian teams struggled to live up to their reputation, blighted by defensive frailties and internal rows. It was not until 1994 that they next appeared in a final, defeating Italy on penalties in a low-key affair to collect a fourth World Cup. But it was hardly vintage Brazil.

Léonidas, Garrincha, Pele, Zico – Brazil had always possessed one true star and in 1998 it was expected to be the turn of Ronaldo. The omens were good until Ronaldo was mysteriously taken ill just before the final. He played but was a shadow of his normal self and France ran out the comfortable 3-0 winners.

In 2002 there was a very real fear that Brazil might fail to qualify for the finals for the first time in their history. However, Luiz Felipe Scolari's team rallied just in time to reach Japan and Korea. There, Ronaldo restored his standing with the two goals that beat Germany in the final. Brazil's captain, Cafu, became the first player to appear in three successive World Cup Finals and Brazil themselves collected the trophy for a record fifth time. The World Cup was back where it belonged.

Brazil 1982. Captained by Socrates (front row, second left) the Brazilians lost out to Italy and a Paolo Rossi hat-trick at the World Cup finals in Spain.

ACKNOWLEDGEMENTS

The following websites proved useful for providing background information for the subjects featured in this book:

International Hall of Fame at www.ifhof.com

Soccer Saints at www.soccersaints.com

FIFA World Cup at www.fifaworldcup.yahoo.com

Roy of the Rovers at www.royoftherovers.com/halloffame

The official websites of Arsenal, Hearts, Liverpool, Manchester City, Manchester United, Scunthorpe United and Spurs

Plus, *The World Encyclopedia of Football* – Tom Macdonald (Lorenz Books, 2001)

Rothmans Football Yearbook (various) – Jack Rollin, Glenda Rollin

EMPICS / Topham Picturepoint
p 92

PA PHOTOS
pp. 6, 7, 8 (below), 9, 10, 11, 12 (below), 15, 16 (below), 17, 18, 20, 23, 24 (below), 25, 27, 28/29 (below), 31, 32, 34 (below), 35, 36, 39, 40, 41(left), 43, 45, 46, 49, 51, 53, 54 (below), 57, 58, 61, 63, 65, 66 (below), 67, 69, 71, 73, 75, 77, 79, 81, 82 (below), 85, 87, 88, 90, 94, 96 (below), 98, 101, 102/103 (below),104, 106, 109, 110, 111

FRONT COVER
© EMPICS: centre below PA PHOTOS: centre, centre left, centre right, below left, below right

BACK COVER
Both pictures: PA PHOTOS